Rethinking Educational Equality

THE NATIONAL SOCIETY
FOR THE STUDY OF EDUCATION

Series on Contemporary Educational Issues
Kenneth J. Rehage, Series Editor

The 1974 Titles

Conflicting Conceptions of Curriculum, Elliot Eisner and Elizabeth
  Vallance, Editors
Crucial Issues in Testing, Ralph W. Tyler and Richard M. Wolf,
  Editors
Cultural Pluralism, Edgar G. Epps, Editor
Rethinking Educational Equality, Andrew Kopan and Herbert
  Walberg, Editors

The National Society for the Study of Education also publishes Year-
books which are distributed by the University of Chicago Press. Inquiries regarding all publications of the Society, as well as inquiries
about membership in the Society, may be addressed to the Secretary-
Treasurer, 5835 Kimbark Avenue, Chicago, 60637.

Rethinking Educational Equality

Edited by

Andrew Kopan
De Paul University
Chicago

and

Herbert Walberg
University of Illinois
Chicago Circle

McCutchan Publishing Corporation
2526 Grove Street
Berkeley, California 94704

ISBN 8211-0012-2
Library of Congress Catalog Card Number 73-20856

© 1974 by McCutchan Publishing Corporation
Printed in the United States of America

Series Foreword

The concept of educational equality appears to have a number of different meanings. In the essays that comprise this volume the authors view the problem of educational equality from different perspectives. Each of these perspectives deserves consideration, and the views expressed here will be useful to the reader who wishes to become familiar with many aspects of this important issue.

The editors of the book, Professors Andrew T. Kopan and Herbert J. Walberg, have given considerable thought to the problem of equality in education. They have organized conferences on the subject at their respective institutions, and some of the papers included here were among those presented at the conferences.

In the current series on Contemporary Educational Issues, *Rethinking Educational Equality* might be regarded as a companion to the volume on *Cultural Pluralism,* edited by Professor Edgar G. Epps. Professor Epps calls upon the schools to be more responsive to diversity in American society and to strive toward goals that accord with the concept of cultural pluralism. Basic to that effort is the notion of equality in education.

The series on Contemporary Educational Issues is published under the auspices of the National Society for the Study of Education. Other titles appearing in this series in 1974 are:

Crucial Issues in Testing, edited by Ralph W. Tyler and Richard M. Wolf;

Conflicting Conceptions of Curriculum, edited by Elliot Eisner and Elizabeth Vallance

With the publication of these four volumes the National Society continues a program begun in 1971 and designed to bring out timely books that provide a background for informed discussion of critical issues in education.

The Society expresses its appreciation to Andrew Kopan and Herbert Walberg, and to the other contributors to this volume, for their efforts in making this interesting collection of essays available.

Kenneth J. Rehage

for the Committee on the Expanded
Publication Program of the
National Society for the Study
of Education

Preface

The public school system has been so much a part of the American ideal of democracy and equality that little attention has been given to the wide differences in educational opportunities that have existed in this country for approximately 250 years. It was not until the civil rights movement and the desegregation controversy following in the wake of the Supreme Court decision in 1954 in *Brown* v. *Board of Education of Topeka* (347 U.S. 483), that educational inequality, especially as reflected among American Negroes and disadvantaged minority groups, received special attention. A growing awareness of economic and social differences and the rise of ethnic identity among minority groups roused efforts to deal with this concern. The Great Society proposed by President Johnson produced many and varied programs to ameliorate inequality among American citizens, and there were some education-oriented ones. In the past decade educational literature has been replete with suggestions of how to bring about equality of educational opportunity in the nation's schools.

After the publication of the well-known Coleman Report of 1966, it became increasingly apparent that the solutions offered under the Great Society program to bring about educational equality in the schools would not suffice. Since the days of Thomas Jefferson it has been assumed by many that education is a means of achieving equality in our society. This assumption has been questioned in recent years by such social scientists as Jencks, Moynihan, Coleman, Jensen, Pettigrew, Herrnstein, and Armor, among others, and it has led to serious disagreement and renewed controversy. Godfrey Hobson's "Do Schools Make a Difference?" (*The Atlantic* 231 [March 1973], 35-46) gives an overview of their work.

Similarly, Horace Mann's belief during the early years of the development of the public schools, that the public schools would be "the equalizers of the conditions of men," facilitating the movement of the poor and disadvantaged into the mainstream of American economic and social life, has likewise come under attack. Contemporary critics such as Michael Katz, Colin Greer and Joel Spring have fostered a revisionist history of education. Their research suggests that school, far from being "the great equalizer," may help to perpetuate differences or, at best, do little to reduce them. They argue that the schools serve the favored few and do not help the poor. They hold that our educational system is harmful to children and that the oppressiveness of the system is neither accidental nor an unforeseen consequence of once noble reform, but that, rather, it reflects the values of a bureaucratic, inegalitarian society. For an excellent analysis and critique of the work of these revisionist historians, see Marvin Lazerson's "Revisionism and American Educational History" (*Harvard Educational Review* 43 [May 1973], 269-83).

The results of revisionist history make it apparent that the issue of educational equality is far from settled and that much "rethinking" of the many-faceted aspects of the problem is in order. If the United States is to become a truly just and humane society, the schools will have to do a better job of educating youngsters from minority-group and lower-class homes. The essays in this volume are addressed to this concern. The authors take the critical approach to education advocated by Henry J. Perkinson in his *The Possibilities of Error: An Approach to Education* (New York: David McKay Company, Inc., 1971). This approach argues that the improvement of education requires a critical strategy. Its foundation is the admission of human fallibility, which allows us to recognize that our present educational situation is not perfect and at the same time to recognize that we can improve it—through criticism, investigation, and change. Accordingly, the purpose of this work is to encourage a reassessment of the problem of educational equality in terms of its economic, sociological, psychological, and philosophical dimensions.

It may be helpful to the reader if he keeps several questions in mind. These questions, though only a few of the many that might be raised, suggest the range of issues that concern the authors and that lie at the heart of problems facing educators.

1. What is the meaning of "educational equality"? Does it concern equality of opportunity or equality of results? How can the extent of equality be measured?
2. What is the purpose of the school with respect to equality? Should the school attempt to foster the equality of students' subsequent incomes? Should it foster nationalism and the common American heritage, or an awareness of the student's own ethnicity and an appreciation of cultural diversity?
3. What consequences follow from answers given to the questions of definition and purpose? How should the schools be changed? Who should be the primary decision makers? What is the proper role of the federal government? How would society reflect educational changes?

The volume begins with Allan Ornstein's "An Overview of the Disadvantaged: 1900-1970." The author presents an analysis of the issue of inequality, noting the different problems confronting European immigrants as compared with the problems faced by racial minority groups later. Early important books of the 1940's, which were concerned with the relationship between social class and education and presaged the current interest in educational equality, are noted. The subsequent development of the issue of educational equality, spearheaded by the civil rights movement and the war on poverty, is analyzed in the light of the seminal writings of Conant, Riessman, and Sexton during the 1960's. Ornstein concludes by identifying eleven general themes that pervaded the literature of educational equality in the past decade and eleven areas of concern for the future.

Herbert Walberg and Mark Bargen give six definitions of educational equality. They show how financial, resource, ethnic, and achievement data may be analyzed and mapped in a large urban area so as to provide indexes of educational equality. Their data indicate resource inequalities within a large district (Chicago), but they also note that variation in educational quality within Illinois and other states is likely to be far larger from one district to another (especially urban and rural districts as contrasted with suburban districts), than within districts.

Henry Levin, in "Distribution of Expenditures," acknowledges that, while our society may lack a strong commitment to equal educational financing, it is now technically possible to specify how expenditures may be more fairly distributed. Using the notion of "human capital embodiment," he argues that the equalization of investment in rich and poor children, not only with respect to education but with respect to housing, health, and family welfare as well, would require vast public expenditures. Levin describes a statewide educational finance plan that provides a compensatory differential for the disadvantaged.

In "Assimilation, Pluralism, and Separatism," Edgar Epps describes a number of forces affecting equality of education for blacks. He shows how Coleman's five conceptions of inequality apply to the black experience and discusses new developments in community control and education for liberation. While reserving final judgment on the best solutions to the problem of black miseducation, Epps emphasizes self-determination and preparation for an urban technological society.

Richard Kolm postulates that lack of recognition of the ethnic identity of a child may cause serious disturbances in personality development and may negatively affect learning capacity, thus contributing to inequality. On the other hand, recognition of ethnic identities of children and a conscious use of ethnic learning patterns can lead to beneficial results in personality and intellectual achievement. He asserts that ethnic studies in schools contribute to the development of a positive self-concept among children and to the improvement of learning, thus enhancing educational equality.

Don Martin and Robert Morgart, in "The Federal Politics of Bussing," discuss the relevance of bussing to educational equality in its national political context. Despite some studies which show that bussing benefits educational equality, the Nixon administration stands opposed to it for economic and political reasons. The authors conclude that, if we are to move away from inequality in our schools to a meaningful degree of equality, provisions must be made for significant social-class integration in the public schools, and the only immediate means appears to be by bussing.

Some contemporary writers conclude that quality of education makes very little difference in society. It might be deduced that, if quality makes little difference, we should not have to worry about equality. The next three articles take issue with this view.

Robert Havighurst, in "Opportunity, Equity, or Equality," summarizes and criticizes the recent Christopher Jencks book on *Inequality*. In contrast to the position of most educational "liberals," who believe schools promote opportunity for the poor, and the position of the "revisionists," who argue that schools deny opportunity to the disadvantaged, Jencks holds that schools make little difference in the economic mobility of the poor and suggests a socialist scheme for direct redistribution of wealth. Havighurst takes a liberal stance and proposes a different analysis of the contribution of education to a number of individual goals.

Mary Jean Bowman's chapter concerns the present dramatic increase in the number of students attending secondary schools and universities. From an economic perspective, she questions conventional wisdom on a number of issues related to equality. For example, she holds that making higher education free does not enlarge freedom of choice and argues that "social demand" is a private affair. A number of studies carried out in the United States, Japan, and Western Europe strengthen these points.

Hans Schieser questions the validity of the phrase "all men are created equal" in light of the vast individual differences among men. For him, it is the distinction between the physical "individual" and the metaphysical "person" that lends meaning to "equality." The original idea of the "United States of America" as a haven for those who sought to be different has been perverted by emphasis on equality over freedom. Schieser sees a reaction to this perversion in the reawakening ethnic awareness and romanticism, and he concludes that there cannot be equality without freedom.

And, in the concluding article, R. Freeman Butts believes that the developments of the 1960's and 1970's have tended to undermine the sense of community, the building of which he believes to be the essential purpose of public education. He draws a distinction between diversity and divisiveness and advocates a restrengthening of the commitment of the public schools to the goals of civic unity. He also calls for a cultural atmosphere in which students may learn the meaning of "mutual dignity, acceptance and self-respect across social and ethnic lines."

Several of the chapters in this volume were originally presented at panel discussions on the topic of educational equality at annual meetings of the American Educational Studies Association (Washington, D.C., November 1972) and the American Educational Research Association (New Orleans, February 1973). Other papers were presented at a joint two-part lecture series on Equality of Educational Opportunity at the University of Illinois, Chicago Circle, on May 12, 1972, and at De Paul University on May 19, 1972.

The editors wish to thank the contributors and to express their appreciation to Kenneth J. Rehage, Robert J. Havighurst, and Edgar G. Epps for their editorial advice in the selection and review of manuscripts.

Andrew T. Kopan
Herbert J. Walberg

Contributors

Mark Bargen, Research Analyst, University of Connecticut

Mary Jean Bowman, Professor of Economics and Education, University of Chicago

R. Freeman Butts, Professor of Education, Teachers College, Columbia University

Edgar G. Epps, Marshall Field Professor of Education, University of Chicago

Robert J. Havighurst, Professor of Education and Human Development, University of Chicago

Richard Kolm, Associate Professor, School of Social Service, Catholic University of America

Andrew T. Kopan, Assistant Professor of Education, De Paul University, Chicago

Henry M. Levin, Associate Professor of Education, Stanford University

Don T. Martin, Assistant Professor of Education, University of Pittsburgh

Robert Morgart, Teaching Associate, School of Education, University of Pittsburgh

Allan C. Ornstein, Associate Professor of Education, Loyola University, Chicago

Hans A. Schieser, Associate Professor of Education, De Paul University, Chicago

Herbert J. Walberg, Research Professor of Urban Education, University of Illinois, Chicago Circle

Contents

1. An Overview of the Disadvantaged: 1900–1970

Allan C. Ornstein

Although the term "disadvantaged" is relatively new, the concern for the people to which it refers dates back to the late nineteenth century, when the immigrants from southern and eastern Europe began their voyage to the promised land.

At that time one of the major aims of the school was to assimilate the immigrants and especially to teach them the language and the democratic concepts for responsible citizenry. Concurrent with the developing need for citizenship training was the view that education was a means to upward mobility. A concept of the school evolved: The school worked for the immigrants and helped them move into the mainstream. Today the feeling is prevalent that the schools have failed the newcomers to the cities—people of rural background, especially blacks from the South.

It is ironical that the school, the so-called savior of the poor, has served as the conveyor belt which has solidified social stratification. Upward mobility was and still is possible only if the student conformed to the schools' middle-class values and expectations. Poor and minority-group children have always found it hard to adapt to the rules of the school. To win favor of those in charge, they have

Reprinted with permission from *Illinois Schools Journal* 52 (Fall-Winter 1972), 51-58. Published by Chicago State University.

had to change their values, habits, and life styles—and only a few are able or feel it necessary to play by these foreign rules.

Most of us fail to recognize that the schools have not educated the children of the poor and immigrants. The schools have actually been a revolving door—the dropout rate before World War I was more than 90 percent. Yet there was not the urgency to do anything for the disadvantaged that there is now, although the dropout rate has decreased to slightly more than one-half. Previously the schools' failure had fewer socioeconomic consequences, and it went largely unnoticed. The unsuccessful school products could still find success within the larger society; they did not face racial discrimination, and they were absorbed into the labor market, which had need for unskilled workers. Thus the immigrants were able to assimilate into the American mainstream in two or three generations. Today's newcomer to the city faces racial discrimination from which he cannot escape no matter how much money he earns. Even worse, the newcomer who drops out of school faces, in addition to discrimination, a restricted job market—one which has little need for unskilled workers. It also takes more education to obtain the same dream, and with the exception of a few "exhibits" the majority of blacks still need more education to obtain the same goals as whites. The economic system limits the number of good jobs, it perpetuates a class society, and it is convenient to subjugate a racial group to a subclass. Thus blacks find it difficult to be integrated into Mainstream, U.S.A., even five generations after the issues of "equality" and "full citizenship" were supposedly decided.

The magnitude of the newcomers' problems was increased by the widening gap between the poor and the middle class and the increased polarization of blacks and whites. This gap has become increasingly visible and intensified by the media, thus fostering increased psychological deprivation and alienation.

Another major difference between the immigrant groups was that the Europeans preserved and perpetuated their own culture and identity, which in turn served as a unifying spirit and catalyst in the social, political, and economic spheres of life. It was this group feeling that helped the immigrants organize and exert political pressure for purposes of social and economic improvement. For example, it was political power that helped bring the sanitation trucks daily into the Jewish or Italian ghetto. It created jobs in local government and made possible neighborhood businesses such as the kosher restaurant and Italian bakery and even clothing stores patronized by the ethnic group of the owner. The immigrants did not have to voice Jewish or Italian power; they secured power through group unity and determination. Blacks today demand economic and political power; therefore, conflict results because those in power (the descendants of the European immigrants) do not readily give up power; it must be taken from them.

During the Depression, there was a temporary exclusion from the good things of life. Deprivation and poverty were not considered permanent or hereditary for most of the poor. With few exceptions there was a sense of hope that things would shortly improve. The popular culture reflected the experience of being poor, and the government official reassured the people that things were improving. Indeed, Eddie Cantor was telling the people that since potatoes were cheaper, "Now's the Time to Fall in Love." President Roosevelt was giving his radio fireside chats, and the New Deal legislation affected almost everyone. At that time, then, it was usual to be poor, and the country was going through a cyclical poverty. Today the poverty is structural—meaning that there are few chances to escape from it, even with individual assistance; moreover, it is out of style to be poor.

While the government was repairing the Depression economy, the assistance was directed at the middle class: the skilled worker, big farmer, small pensioner, and small businessman. Except for the emergency relief agencies very little help was given to those who would coincide with today's structural poor—migrant farmers, Okies, blacks; they were silent and invisible, hidden in rural wastelands from the American ear and eye.

By the 1940's the concern for color and caste was evident at least in the academic community. A few of the classic studies are worth mentioning. The relationship between social class and education and the ways in which the lower class was penalized in schools were shown by Warner *et al., Who Shall Be Educated* (1944); Davis, *Social Class Influences upon Learning* (1948); and Hollingshead, *Elmtown's Youth* (1949). The social, economical, and political problems of blacks and the ways in which racial discrimination and segregation were related to these problems were shown by Davis and Dollard, *Children of Bondage* (1940); Drake and Cayton, *Black Metropolis* (1945); and Myrdal, *American Dilemma* (1944).

It was not until the early 1960's that there was interest on a national level in the poor, especially the black poor, as a result of the civil rights movement and subsequent war on poverty. The fact that racism accommodated the nation's needs, coupled with the fact that racism is a contradiction of the American slogans of "liberty, justice, and equality" and that it contradicts the concept of the melting pot, had caused white America to avoid the reality of and direct dealing with the social process. Also, the fact that poverty is an obvious, crushing contradiction in American life escaped widespread public concern until this fact surfaced suddenly in the American consciousness.

The civil rights movement, spearheaded by Dr. Martin Luther King, Jr., exposed white prejudices and discrimination. It was nonviolence, not black power or race riots, that caused white anxiety and white violence to appear. The peaceful civil rights movement preceded Stokely Carmichael and Watts. Today, however, white racism and the directly related rise of black racism among a small group now confront each other and threaten the social fabric of the country.

Harrington's *The Other America* (1963) was essential in sparking the war on poverty and subsequent related federal programs for the education of the children of the poor and minorities. Not since Dickens had someone captured the problems and life styles of the poor, but this time the poor that were being described were Americans. Harrington estimated that there were between forty and fifty million Americans who lived in poverty, and the type of poverty was hereditary or structural. Although the number of poor was challenged by numerous authorities and councils—including the government, which contended there were between thirty and thirty-five million poor Americans—Harrington's point was that a piecemeal, individual case approach could not solve the problem; massive funds and a full-scale program were needed. The problem was not only blacks but also poor whites; poor whites were just as much a minority group. Because they were white, they were invisible, and nobody paid much attention to them. Indeed, Harrington directly struck at the American conscience by declaring that the poor were the victims of our affluent, industrial society; moreover, he charged for the first time that a society had the material ability to end poverty but lacked the will to do so.

In the meantime, educators began to reflect the nation's concern over the twin problems of race and poverty and the fear of a possible conflict between the haves and have nots, especially between whites and blacks. Educators focused on the children of the poor, blacks, and other minorities with such euphemisms as the disadvantaged, deprived, and underprivileged. The classification of "cultural deprivation" was added to the *Educational Index,* beginning with 21 entries in Volume 13, July 1961-June 1963; by Volume 15, July 1964-June 1965, the number had increased to 122 entries; by Volume 19, July 1968-June 1969, the most recently completed volume at the time of this writing, the number was 370 with several other similar headings such as city schools, cultural difference, poverty, Negro, etc. It is with this period, from the beginning of the 1960's to the present, that the rest of this paper will be concerned, and an attempt will be made to synthesize the literature.

Perhaps the three books that presaged the field and had the greatest impact were Conant's *Slums and Suburbs* (1961), Riessman's *The Culturally Deprived Child* (1962), and Sexton's *Education and Income* (1964).

Conant, in a rather cursory and undocumented form, compared the slum schools and slum students with their respective counterparts in suburbia. He coined the term "social dynamite" and warned that conditions were reaching an intolerable and explosive point in the ghettoes of the cities. The prestige and influence of Conant was a major factor in awakening educators and other responsible citizens to the plight of the slum school.

Riessman, at that time a relatively unknown psychologist from Bard College, became the number one expert in the field as a result of his book, which was published as a sleeper, but reached the market at the right time. Riessman helped people understand the problems of educating the disadvantaged. Although he tended to romanticize the disadvantaged, even to the point of comparing their mental styles to that of true genius, he clearly showed that the disadvantaged had their own culture and that this culture was in conflict with the schools' middle-class values. He went on to list several suggestions for classroom teachers, which were fundamental and practical. Until the end of the decade, almost all subsequent books on the subject referred to or cited the book; at this time (1971) the book has gone through twelve printings.

Sexton statistically showed the lack of equal educational opportunity for low-income youth and the numerous discriminatory characteristics of the low-income schools' physical plant, staff, and resources in comparison with higher-income schools. For nearly every school characteristic, Sexton showed that advantage was positively correlated with the median income of the students' parents. The results were not earthshaking, but actually a confirmation of sociological wisdom which dated back at least to the Lynd study of *Middletown* (1929). What Sexton did, however, was to show how income is related to educational opportunity with the use of simple statistics accompanied by a readable discussion, so that the average reader could understand the significance of the study. Another intangible variable was contemporary history; this time educators, government officials, and citizens were willing to listen. Therefore, by the end of the decade most of the low-income schools, at least in the northern cities, equalized or more than equalized most of the characteristics described in the study through extra money and special programs. However, important characteristics which probably have not been equalized are the teachers' attitudes, behavior, and morale —all of which are extremely difficult to change and have very little to do with the amount of money a school spends on programs for educating its students.

By the mid-sixties interest in the disadvantaged had reached the bandwagon status. Several of the educational journals had already published or were soon to publish feature issues on the disadvantaged. The increasing amount of research in the field led the *Review of Educational Research* to devote their October 1965 issue to the subject. The same year, one of the nineteen ERIC [Educational Resources Information Center] clearinghouses founded by the U. S. Office of Education was dedicated to the disadvantaged to collect and disseminate the rapidly proliferating reports and studies on the subject. The ERIC file accumulated several thousand reports and studies on the same subject in their *Office of Educational Reports,* 1956-65, and in 1965 *Research in Education,* a monthly index, was published and still continues monthly listings on the disadvantaged.

Training programs for teachers of the disadvantaged and related courses and advanced degrees in the field began to appear across the country. Corresponding to the increased concern for educating teachers for the disadvantaged was a surge of conferences, position papers, and books on the subject, not to mention the growth of journals, articles, and research studies in the field, most of which regurgitated nearly the same wisdom and tired statements of what was wrong along with suggested solutions based on hunches, sentiment, and unverified or subjective data.

Regurgitation was also pervasive among most of the experts. Because of space limitations, only a few examples will be given here. Some writers merely lifted whole sections or major portions of one manuscript and transformed them to another manuscript, revised or updated the same discussion and organized it under different titles.

Edmond Gordon reviewed basically the same compensatory programs under different subheadings in at least four different publications.[1] Robert Havighurst repeated the same theme about the characteristics of the disadvantaged in three manuscripts.[2] Irwin Katz mainly reviewed psychological problems of black children and youth in four studies.[3] Frank Riessman discussed the disadvantaged child's mental styles and physical and hidden verbal ability in at least nine different sources.[4] J. M. Hunt repeated the same discussion about the different views of intelligence and the need for environmental stimulation in at least three different sources.[5]

Viewing the entire decade as an entity, the literature centered on eleven general themes:

1. Descriptions and characteristics of the disadvantaged—mainly in sociopsychological and racial terms, with a prevailing negative image.
2. Concern over achievement, reading, and intelligence tests, with general agreement that they discriminated against the disadvantaged.
3. Descriptions and evaluations of compensatory programs, with special emphasis on both extremes of the educational continuum —prekindergarten and college. Most of the programs were considered ineffective.
4. Descriptions and characteristics of teachers of the disadvantaged, mainly in terms of negative attitudes and behavior and limited experience.
5. Concern over instructional techniques for the disadvantaged, which could be lumped under good teaching for all children, but more necessary for the disadvantaged.
6. Descriptions and evaluations of teacher-training programs, most

of which were judged to emphasize theory and de-emphasize practice. Training of local residents as paraprofessionals and eventually as teachers of the disadvantaged.

7. Methods for recruiting teachers of the disadvantaged, with emphasis on assigning qualified teachers to ghetto schools.
8. The growth of teacher unions in city schools, and especially in the ghetto areas where teacher morale is low.
9. Concern over curriculum reform, with emphasis on relevant materials, developing language and cognitive skills, improving the image of minorities in textbooks and quality of integrated primers, and revising the content so that it portrays a more realistic role of minorities.
10. Descriptions of the schools serving the disadvantaged, negatively portrayed—and the effects of segregated and integrated schools on black students.
11. Concern over school reorganization and providing alternative schemes for educating the disadvantaged, including state and federal subsidies for students.

At the time of this writing, the direction and problems of the 1970's also seem to be concerned with:

1. Teacher accountability and teacher-behavior models and learning theories applicable for working with the disadvantaged.
2. Possible elimination of merit pay and promotion based on formal examinations, and increased preferential hiring and promoting of minority-group school personnel in black and other minority group schools.
3. Increased use of sensitivity training for school personnel.
4. Concern over reduced governmental and school-system spending on all educational programs, with a ripple of concern for the disadvantaged.
5. Renewed interest in behavioral objectives for teaching the disadvantaged.
6. Community action-related educational and health programs.
7. Increased open enrollment at the college level, at city and state institutions, and special educational and financial assistance for the disadvantaged.
8. Increased black-white racism in schools and communities, with special emphasis for local control by a vocal minority of blacks, and special concern by whites to maintain neighborhood schools.

9. A subsystems approach to educating the disadvantaged, including governmental, business, scientific, and cultural agencies.
10. Institutes to combat racism.
11. The role of the social scientist, and the merits of reporting research that negatively depicts an ethnic or racial group, and the right for free inquiry in such sensitive areas.

Reflecting upon the last decade, educators came to realize that they lacked answers. Little has been definite and consistent, excepting the obvious, e.g., poor students have lower achievement grades than middle-class students. The lack of our knowledge seemed to be partially due to the fact that variables and subsequent results varied because they were functional to varied situations. As the complexity of the problems became evident, the old truism became applicable to the field: we were only at the first stage of wisdom, the humble confession of how little we know. Rather than formulate ideas and programs that were based on hunches, we now have come to the realization that we first have to find what can work, with whom, to what extent, under what conditions.

Notes

1. Edmund Gordon, "A Review of Programs of Compensatory Education," *American Journal of Orthopsychiatry* 35 (July 1965), 644-51; *id.* and Doxey A. Wilkerson, *Compensatory Education for the Disadvantaged* (New York: College Entrance Examination Board, 1966); *id.*, "Programs of Compensatory Education," in Martin Deutsch *et al.* (eds.), *Social Class, Race, and Psychological Development* (New York: Holt, 1968), 381-410; *id.* and Adelaide Jablonsky, "Compensatory Education in the Equalization of Educational Opportunity," *Journal of Negro Education* 37 (Summer 1968), 268-79.

2. Robert J. Havighurst, "Who are the Disadvantaged?" *Journal of Negro Education* 33 (Summer 1964) 210-17, "Social Backgrounds: Their Impact on School Children," in Thomas D. Horn (ed.), *Reading for the Disadvantaged* (New York: Harcourt, 1970), 11-20, and "Minority Subcultures and the Law of Effect," *American Psychologist* 25 (April 1970), 313-22.

3. Irwin Katz, "Review of Evidence Relating to Effects of Desegregation on the Intellectual Performance of Negroes," *American Psychologist* 19 (June 1964), 381-99, "Desegregation or Integration in Public Schools? The Policy Implications of Research," *Integrated Education* 5 (1967-68), 15-27, "Factors Influencing Negro Performance in the Desegregated School," in Martin Deutsch *et al.* (eds.), *op. cit.*, 254-89, and "A Critique of Personality Approaches to Negro Performance, with Research Suggestions," *Journal of Social Issues* 25 (January 1969), 13-27.

4. Frank Riessman, *The Culturally Deprived Child* (New York: Harper, 1962), "Culturally Deprived Child: A New View," *School Life* 45 (April 1963), 5-7, "Overlooked Positives of Disadvantaged Groups," *Journal of Negro Education* 33 (Summer 1964), 225-31, "The Strategy of Style," *Teachers College Record* 65 (March 1964), 484-89, "Low Income Culture, the Adolescent, and the School," *Bulletin of the National Association of Secondary School Principals* 49 (April 1965), 45-49, "Styles of Learning," *NEA Journal* 55 (March 1966), 15-17, *Helping the Disadvantaged Pupil to Learn More Easily* (Englewood Cliffs, N.J.: Prentice-Hall, 1966), "Teachers of the Poor: A Five Point Plan," *Journal of Teacher Education* 18 (Fall 1967), 326-36, and "Further Thoughts on Educating the Disadvantaged," in A. Harry Passow (ed.), *Developing Programs for the Educationally Disadvantaged* (New York: Teachers College, Columbia University, 1967).

5. J. M. Hunt, *Intelligence and Experience* (New York: Ronald, 1961), "The Psychological Basis for Using Pre-school Enrichment as an Antidote for Cultural Deprivation," *Merrill-Palmer Quarterly* 10 (July 1964), 209-48, and "How Children Develop Intellectually," *Children* 11 (May-June 1964), 83-91.

2. Equality: Operational Definitions and Empirical Tests

Herbert J. Walberg and *Mark Bargen*

Since *The Republic,* men have argued over the definition and provision of quality education in a good society. Plato, it will be re-
called, devoted much of his dialectic to specifying the conditions of
education that produce excellent individuals for a just state. But he
was also concerned with a second ideal—equality of opportunity; and
he pointed out that children of gold are sometimes produced by
parents of brass and that educators should identify and nurture them
to join the ranks of philosopher kings. As shown by de Tocqueville's
Democracy in America[1] and Myrdal's *An American Dilemma,*[2] no
country has taken the second ideal more seriously, continuously, or
with greater anguish than our own. Yet we still have far to go in
providing quality and equality in American education.

The empirical researcher, faced with a host of philosophical, legal,
polemical, and romantic concepts of educational equality, must attempt to develop measures of the concepts to evaluate school equality. Like the astronomer who cannot clearly observe all he wishes, let
alone manipulate the heavens, the educational research worker must
work cautiously with measures of schools that are imperfect opera-

Reprinted from Herbert J. Walberg (ed.), *Evaluating Educational Performance:
A Sourcebook of Methods, Instruments, and Examples* (Berkeley, Calif.:
McCutchan Publishing Corporation, 1974), 223-38.

Table 2-1. Concepts of educational equality

Definition	Problems
1. *Negative:* quality of education does not depend on individual, social, ethnic, or other characteristics of the student or where he happens to receive his education.	What is "educational quality?" What should be equalized: individual, class, school, district, city, or state education?
2. *Political:* appointed or elected individuals representative of all majorities and minorities have equal control over resources and quality.	A definition of decision making rather than concept. What groups should be represented: social, ethnic, or geographical? What unit should they control: school, district, city, or state?
3. *Racial:* integrate racial or ethnic groups in unit of geographical area.	Little consistent evidence of racial inequalities in resources within certain geographical areas. Little consistent evidence that racial segregation in schools is harmful by itself. May discourage cultural pluralism. Expense and public resistance to bussing. How define groups and areas?
4. *Socioeconomic:* integrate socioeconomic groups within unit of geographical area.	Same problems as racial definition except that there is some moderately creditable evidence that socioeconomic integration can help lower socioeconomic groups.
5. *Economic:*	Assumes expenditures determine educational quality.
a. Utopian: continue to allocate additional funds to each student until additional increments produce no gains.	Economic limitations of society or higher priorities for other social and individual goals.
b. Minimum: establish minimum expenditure level; state supplies funds to localities that cannot supply minimum; willing districts can spend more than minimum.	Amount spent still depends on place of residence.
c. Egalitarian: spend more on lower ability students so that all students leave school with an equal chance for success.	How measure ability? May be relatively poor social investment. Is the purpose of the school to compensate for inequalities? Can it? May discourage excellence.

d. Elite: spend more on higher ability students since they may benefit more from scarce resources and later contribute more to social quality and equality.

    How measure ability? May further enrich the advantaged.

e. Financial: spend equal funds on each student.

    Costs may vary for different children and in different parts of the state.

f. Maximum Variance: set limit on ratio of expenditures for education in high and low districts, e.g. 1½ to 1.

    May curb local initiative.

g. Classification: equal treatment of equals; expenditures assigned to students on the basis of statewide classifications, such as "creative" and "blind."

    How classify students?

6. *Resource:* use any of the economic variants except school resources such as physical plant, teacher qualifications, and library books as the units of allocation or equalization rather than expenditures.

    Measureable resources may not determine quality of education.

*Adapted and synthesized from: A. E. Wise, *Rich Schools, Poor Schools: The Promise of Equal Educational Opportunity* (Chicago: University of Chicago Press, 1968); and M. T. Katzman, *The Political Economy of Urban Schools* (Cambridge, Mass.: Harvard University Press, 1971).

tional representations of abstract concepts. The main intent of this chapter is to analyze such measures and show their spatial distribution in the Chicago Public Schools. Before doing so, however, the underlying concepts are set forth and critically examined.

Apparently only two writers, Wise and Katzman[3] have tried to draw up comprehensive lists of definitions of educational equality. Their lists do not overlap completely, and we have synthesized their definitions in Table 2-1. Among the six definitions and twelve variants, the first one, the negative, raises the least dissent because it is the most abstract; however, it is nearly useless for generating a measure of equality. The second column of Table 2-1 lists the problems encountered with each of the definitions. The political, racial, and socioeconomic definitions force us to categorize people in ways that are not only unacceptable to many but also impractical to carry out in attaining equality. Would we equate a Negro or white immigrant from rural Mississippi or Appalachia with a member of an established Negro or white Chicago family in composing the Chicago school board? Should Latins and Orientals be integrated with whites or Negroes? Or, indeed, is the term "Oriental" adequate in view of the cultural differences among Chinese, Japanese, and Koreans? Difficulties are also encountered with the economic and resource definitions, as shown in Table 2-1. Moreover, problems and costs in obtaining measurements would still exist even if the definitions were entirely acceptable.

Perhaps the only way to obtain indubitable equality is to provide no education at all, or to devise a programmed machine that would completely control each child's environment from birth. Because these alternatives are unacceptable, and because imperfect concepts and limited information are generally better than none at all in reaching a conclusion, we turn to an analysis of some national, state, and large-city data on educational equality.

Table 2-2 shows "coefficients of variation," indexes calculated by dividing the standard deviation by the mean, that measure the variation in expenditure or resource distribution from the arithmetic average. If there is no variation, the coefficient will be zero; if there is large variation, the index will approach unity. This index is superior to the range or ratio of highest to lowest unit that has been used in popular accounts of expenditure inequalities because it takes into account the entire distribution of all units rather than the two most extreme.

Table 2-2. Coefficients of variation (inequalities) for providing education at several levels

| | Total | Interstate | Intrastate | Intracity | | | | |
				1967 Atlanta	1971 Boston	1967 Chicago	1971 Chicago
Expenditures per student	.72	.25	.24	.14	.13	.15	.08
Teacher Education	.48	—	.21	—	.23	.26	.15
Teacher Experience	.40	—	.60	.25	.24	.69	.27
Class Size	.26	—	.18	.11	.24	.05	.06

Note. The figures in the first six columns are adapted from those compiled from several sources by M. T. Katzman in *The Political Economy of the Urban Schools* (Cambridge, Mass.: Harvard University Press, 1971), pp. 120 and 136.

The first row of coefficients shows that inequalities in total expenditures per student are far larger in schools across the nation, across states, and within states than they are within the three large cities sampled. These figures suggest that the largest inequalities in student expenditures are among states and among school districts within states rather than within large cities. This hypothesis is further supported by scattered evidence[4] that student expenditures are generally highest in wealthy, highly industrialized states and in affluent suburban districts.

Consider the large city inequalities in expenditures per student. Three major studies have been conducted. Sexton[5] reported large inequalities in the Detroit public schools, but did not present figures that can be comprehensively analyzed. Studies by Burkhead, Fox, and Holland[6] of Atlanta and Chicago and by Katzman[7] of Boston revealed relatively small inequalities in total expenditures per student as shown in Table 2-2. Moreover, our analysis of Chicago high school data in the last column shows that total expenditures were more equal in 1971 than in 1967 and that inequalities in teacher education and experience were reduced while variations in class size remained at about the same low level.

Table 2-3 shows some additional measures of inequality for 389 elementary and 46 secondary public schools in Chicago. If racial integration provides equality, the Chicago schools, like those in the rest of the nation,[8] are highly unequal. While the mean percent Negro of elementary schools is 46, 41 percent of the schools are more than 95 percent Negro and 40 percent are more than 95 percent white; and the corresponding coefficient of variation is very high, .99. The same coefficient for high schools is smaller, .89, because these schools have larger attendance boundaries and are therefore more likely to include mixed populations.

The variation coefficients for other indexes of equality in Table 2-3, however, present a different picture. . . .[9] Inequalities in total expenditures, expenditures for regular teachers, mean class size, and mean coded teacher education are relatively small in the elementary and secondary schools. Expenditures for materials are unequal, but they are a small component of total operating expenditures per student. However, mean teacher experience and expenditures for extra personnel (principals, counselors) are unequally distributed in both elementary and secondary schools. Since total expenditures are equal but their components and what they purchase are not, we now turn

Table 2-3. Statistics on the Chicago public schools

	Elementary (N = 389)				Secondary (N = 46)			
	Mean	Standard Deviation	Variation Coefficient	Achievement Correlation	Mean	Standard Deviation	Variation Coefficient	Achievement Correlation
Percent Negro	.46	.46	.99	−.60	.47	.42	.89	−.81
Total expenditures	$472.94	63.10	.13	.30	636.02	51.37	.08	.17
Regular teachers	$367.80	45.00	.12	.41	518.26	40.78	.08	.30
Extra personnel	$91.68	26.96	.29	.02	100.57	19.75	.20	−.16
Materials	$13.46	4.28	.32	.00	17.20	2.42	.14	−.07
Class size	33.48	2.71	.08	.18	23.02	1.47	.06	.51
Teacher education	1.29	.16	.13	.64	1.53	.23	.15	.88
Teacher experience	7.67	2.63	.34	.75	6.77	1.85	.27	.82

to the spatial distribution of separate variables throughout the city (Figures 2-1—2-3).

Figure 2-1 shows the distribution of mean coded teacher education and experience, and mean class size of 389 elementary schools throughout the city. For all computer maps in this chapter, the darker the area, the higher it is (in ten equal intervals) on the variable mapped. The darkness at any particular point depicts the mean value of schools in the immediate area. Figure 2-1 is particularly important because the three resources mapped account for about 80 percent of the operating expenditures of the Chicago public schools and other large school systems in United States. Teacher education and experience and class size show definite spatial patterns. Schools with highly educated, experienced teachers are concentrated in the outlying areas of the city, particularly in the north, northwest, and southwest. Schools with smaller mean class sizes, however, are concentrated in the remaining areas, especially in the inner city and in two sectors extending west and south from the center city. Thus, total operating expenditures per student tend to be equal throughout the city because their two main components, teacher salaries (based on degree and graduate credits attained and years of experience) and class size are traded off in the school system: the inner city, western, and southern sectors get smaller classes; the remaining areas get higher "teacher quality," that is, more experienced, more highly educated teachers. And now, one wonders, which are the areas of higher achievement?

Figure 2-2 shows the distribution of first-grade reading readiness, sixth-grade reading achievement, and the extent to which sixth-grade students outperform or underperform a regression prediction from first-grade readiness scores on students in the same schools. . . .[10] Comparing Figures 2-1 and 2-2 reveals that both higher readiness and achievement and, to a lesser extent, performance are found in areas of higher teacher quality rather than in areas with smaller classes. The achievement correlations in Table 2-3 bear out this pattern: sixth-grade achievement is correlated .64 with teacher education, .75 with experience, and .18 with class size; and the corresponding correlations are even higher in the secondary schools. For example, class size is correlated .51 with eleventh-grade achievement (of course, no causal relations can be safely assumed). From the high negative correlations in Table 2-1 between achievement and percent Negro in the school (−.60 and −.81 for elementary and secondary schools, respec-

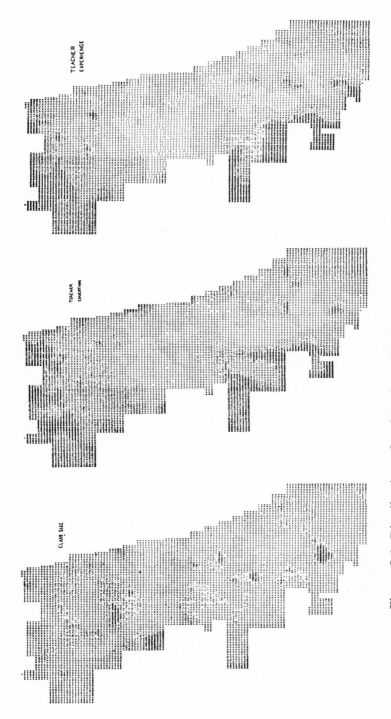

Figure 2-1. Distribution of major educational resources in the Chicago Public Schools

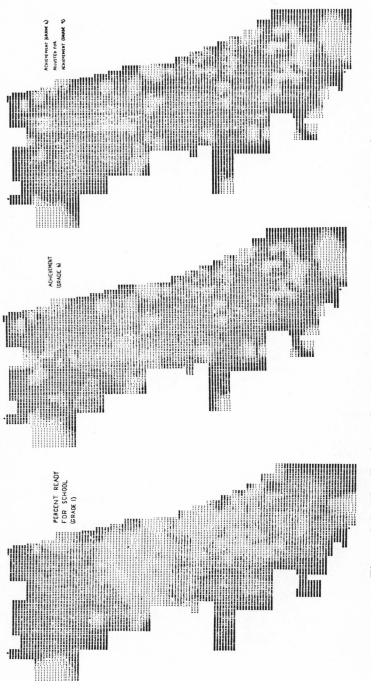

Figure 2-2. Distribution of readiness, achievement, and achievement gains

tively), one might infer that racial percentages are spatially linked to the chain of teacher quality, class size, and achievement.

Figure 2-3 reveals that this is indeed the case. The areas of lower teacher quality, smaller class sizes, and lower achievement in the inner city and southern and western sectors tend to contain schools with more than 95 percent Negro students. The figure also shows the pattern of segregation very clearly: most schools are nearly all Negro or all white. Moreover, the part of the figure showing change in percent Negro from the 1969-70 to 1970-71 school years shows not a random dispersion of Negroes throughout white areas of the city, as some have hoped, but an obvious growth in school percent Negro around the perimeters of the Negro areas. The in-migration of rural southern Negroes to Chicago and the out-migration of middle-class whites to the suburbs, noted for several decades,[11] is apparently continuing, while the city's population has remained fairly constant.

To examine the pattern of expenditures and resources allocated to the main racial-ethnic groups in the city, the 389 schools were divided into five groups, as shown in Table 2-4: 147 schools, in which more than 95 percent of the students were white, were classified as white; 36 predominantly white, 50 to 95 percent; 30 predominantly Negro, 50 to 95 percent; 147 Negro, above 95 percent; and 29 Latin, where this was the largest ethnic group in the school. A multivariate analysis of variance showed that the patterns of allocation are significantly different (probability less than .001) in the five groups of schools, and Table 2-4 shows the group means. As suggested by the spatial patterns on the maps, white schools have higher teacher expenditures and hence more experienced and better-educated staffs, but larger classes. Negro and Latin schools have lower teacher expenditures but smaller class sizes, and slightly higher expenditures on extra personnel.

Finally, let us consider the achievement levels of the five groups of schools on first-grade reading readiness, and fourth- and sixth-grade reading achievement. Table 2-5 shows a pattern of differences that are highly significant (probability less than .001) in a multivariate analysis of variance. In the white schools, an average of about 77 percent of the first graders are "ready" for the school reading program, while in the Negro and Latin schools the corresponding average percentages are 45 and 40, respectively. The large differences among the groups persist on reading tests in the fourth and sixth grades, except that Latin schools outperform Negro schools slightly at the

Figure 2-3. Distribution of Negro enrollment and change in Negro enrollment

Table 2-4. Expenditures and resources for the five groups

School	Expenditures per student				Resources		
	Regular Teachers	Extra Personnel	Materials	Class Size	Teacher Education	Teacher Experience
White	379.40	90.48	13.03	34.43	1.39	9.55
Predominately White	381.14	93.42	14.61	33.32	1.34	8.28
Predominately Negro	368.50	94.07	14.37	33.95	1.26	7.33
Negro	356.26	90.63	13.56	32.45	1.19	6.02
Latin	350.33	96.15	12.59	33.80	1.20	5.89
F-ratios	6.99***	.041	1.69	11.28***	45.00***	59.52***

Note. F-ratios with three asterisks are significant at the .001 level; those with no asterisks are not significant at the .10 level.

Table 2-5. Mean achievement at three grade levels
for five groups of schools

Schools	First-grade reading readiness *(percent ready)*	Fourth-grade reading achievement, National T-scores	Sixth-grade reading achievement, National T-scores
White	76.59	51.54	50.15
Predominantly white	71.33	49.40	48.21
Predominantly Negro	64.53	48.34	46.48
Negro	45.31	44.95	42.53
Latin	39.52	44.28	43.57
F-ratios	66.98	70.22	75.59

Note: All F-ratios are significant beyond the .001 level.

sixth-grade level. Even at these grade levels, however, Latin and Negro schools are about .6 of a standard deviation below white schools in Chicago.

Do the Chicago schools provide educational equality? The answers are complex and depend on one's concept of equality. If equality means racial integration, the answer is no. If it means equal expenditures, the answer is yes. If it means equal resources and reading achievement, the answer is no. As we have shown, white schools in the outlying areas of the city have high achievement levels, large classes, and more experienced, well-educated teachers. In minority schools in the central area and the western and southern sectors, the achievement and school resource pattern is reversed: large percentages of students enter first grade unready for school and, confirming reanalysis of the Coleman data,[12] remain behind in the later grades. Thus the Chicago schools, like others in the nation, do not appear to overcome family origins.

These major findings must be considered with caution. Political. and socioeconomic concepts of educational equality are neglected here; gathering data on these concepts would be a major undertaking and perhaps worthwhile despite our reservations about their definitions in Table 2-1. Moreover, data on only three major racial-ethnic groups—Negroes, Latins, and whites—have been examined; surely there are large differences in social class, cultural, and other characteristics within these groups that might profitably be investigated with respect to educational equality. Limiting the analysis to only one output measure—reading achievement—is unfortunate given the many goals of education, but perhaps inevitable given the limited number of correlated output measures available. Moreover, it should be remembered that inequalities in expenditures and resources in Chicago and other large cities surveyed are small compared to differences between cities and their suburbs and among states.

Even with these cautions in mind, however, the findings may have some substantive and practical implications. It is disturbing that minority groups get lower "teacher quality," even though they are compensated with smaller class sizes, because minority children, particularly Negroes, appear to benefit more than whites from better teachers.[13] No one has defined "good teaching" with scientific rigor, but advanced degrees, recency of education, teaching experience, and verbal aptitude have been fairly consistently associated with student achievement gains in a number of large-scale surveys.[14] Class size, on the other hand, is usually found to be uncorrelated with achievement goals. Like the cancer-smoking correlation, the scientific case for teacher qualities cannot be made without experiments. Yet, even in the face of noncausal evidence, the prudent man reconsiders smoking, and the just society reconsiders the distribution of effective educational resources.

On moral, if not scientific, grounds, then, efforts should be made to equalize teacher quality in Chicago. At least as far back as 1950, ill-prepared novice teachers in Chicago have typically started their careers in the most difficult minority schools.[15] About half, disillusioned and traumatized by the experience,[16] abandon their teaching careers within two years. (Some, of course, leave for other reasons, such as child rearing.) Those who remain are allowed to transfer to higher-achieving schools after several years. These two factors make for very high rates of staff inexperience and mobility in these minority schools, which are also encumbered by many other problems. More seasoned and specially prepared teachers should be brought in to help solve the educational problems of these schools.

In conclusion, three points are worth repeating. The schools as they are presently organized, or as they might be organized with the best research and wisdom we have, cannot compensate for individual, family, and institutional inequalities in the community beyond their control. The Chicago schools provide relatively equal educational opportunity as far as determined here, but the quality of teaching staffs should be more fairly distributed. The large identifiable educational inequalities in our society extend beyond the metropolitan area and are between the city and rural areas of poverty on one hand and the affluent suburbs on the other.

Notes

1. A. de Tocqueville, *Democracy in America* (New York: Alfred A. Knopf, 1946).

2. Gunnar Myrdal, *An American Dilemma: The Negro Problem and Modern Democracy* (New York: Harper, 1944).

3. Arthur E. Wise, *Rich Schools, Poor Schools: The Promise of Equal Educational Opportunity* (Chicago: University of Chicago Press, 1968); M. T. Katzman, *The Political Economy of Urban Schools* (Cambridge, Mass.: Harvard University Press, 1971).

4. Katzman, *op. cit.*

5. P. C. Sexton, *Education and Income: The Inequalities of Opportunity in Our Public Schools* (New York: Viking Press, 1961).

6. J. Burkhead, T. G. Fox, and J. W. Holland, *Input and Output in Large City High Schools* (Syracuse, N. Y.: Syracuse University Press, 1967).

7. Katzman, *op. cit.*

8. J. S. Coleman *et al.*, *Equality of Educational Opportunity* (Washington, D.C.: U.S. Government Printing Office, 1966).

9. Herbert J. Walberg (ed.), *Evaluating Educational Performance: A Sourcebook of Methods, Instruments, and Examples* (Berkeley, Calif.: McCutchan Publishing Corporation, 1974). See ch. 13, Table 2, for further definition of the variables.

10. See *ibid.*, for information on these tests.

11. K. E. Tauber, "The Demographic Context of Metropolitan Education," in J. McV. Hunt (ed.), *Human Intelligence* (New Brunswick, N.J.: Transaction Books, 1972), 77-97.

12. F. W. Mosteller and D. P. Moynihan, *On Equality of Educational Opportunity* (New York: Random House, 1972).

13. *Ibid.*

14. Katzman, *op. cit.*

15. H. S. Becker, "The Career of the Chicago Public School Teacher," *American Journal of Sociology* 57 (March 1952), 470-77.

16. Herbert J. Walberg *et al.*, "Effects of Tutoring and Practice Teaching on Self-Concept and Attitudes in Education Students," *Journal of Teacher Education* 19 (Fall 1968), 283-91.

3. Equal Educational Opportunity and the Distribution of Educational Expenditures

Henry M. Levin

Public educational investment represents the principal method by which our society attempts to equalize opportunity among children born into different circumstances. Given the crucial conceptual role of the educational system, the allocation of public funds for the attainment of equal educational opportunity has become a focal social concern in recent years. In 1971, a landmark decision of the California Supreme Court[1] declared that the present system of financing education "with its substantial dependence on local property taxes and resultant wide disparities in school revenue, violates the equal protection clause of the Fourteenth Amendment . . . because it makes the quality of a child's education a function of the wealth of his parents and neighbors." In rapid succession, the existing schemes for financing education have been overturned by state courts in both Minnesota and New Jersey and by a federal district court in Texas. A rash of similar suits in other states suggests a thorough overhaul of the traditional mechanisms for financing education.

In response, state legislatures and the federal government have initiated a frenzied search for alternatives for supporting the schools.[2] In some states, there are recommendations for a shift to

Reprinted from *Education and Urban Society* 5 (February 1973), 149-72, by permission of the publisher, Sage Publications, Inc.

income and sales taxes, while in others the legislatures are considering statewide, uniform property taxes. There are indications that the
federal government may also get into the act with the President's
announcement in early 1972 that a federal value-added tax is being
studied as a substitute for the school-related property tax levy.[3]

The emphasis in both the legal cases and the recent federal activity
has been on the improvement of equity with regard to the support of
the educational function. That is, the palliatives to the traditional
approach have stressed primarily the criterion of fairness in the underlying system of taxation. Much less research and discussion have
been generated on the optimal distribution of educational investment
among children of social groups. This is especially surprising given
the substantial discussion in recent years on the meaning and implementation of equal educational opportunity among youngsters born
into different circumstances.[4]

The purpose of this paper is to address the distribution and composition of educational investment among social classes. Though a
more equitable educational system might improve relative opportunities among children from modest circumstances, there is abundant
evidence that suggests we cannot and should not rely upon the educational system alone for this task. Even with the same nominal
amounts of schooling, it appears that nonwhites earn considerably
less than whites and that persons from lower socioeconomic origins
show lower occupational and income attainments than persons from
higher origins.[5] Whether this is due to discrimination or to a class
structure that reproduces itself is beyond the scope of this study.[6]
Yet, it is important to assert at the outset that educational reform is
not a substitute for social reform, although the former can certainly
be an integral part of the latter.[7]

Equality of Educational Opportunity

Any attempt to equalize educational opportunity must begin with
the rationale for doing so. Definitions of equal educational opportunity such as "equal access to education," or "enabling each child
to maximize his potential" abound in the educational literature, but
they offer little insight into educational policy. Both of these suffer
from ambiguity since they are subject to a wide variety of interpretations. Moreover, what applications are attempted tend to define edu-

cation as only *formal schooling,* despite the plethora of educational experiences and influences that take place outside the schools.

If we return to the origins of the American public schools, we see that the discussion and ferment that led to universal public schooling was heavily dominated by the conception that education was the best path to "equal opportunity." Indeed the rise of the "common school" is associated with the often-quoted statement by Horace Mann: "Education, then, beyond all other devices of human origin, is the great equalizer of the conditions of men—the balance-wheel of the social machinery."[8]

This movement did not represent a quest for a classless society as much as it reflected a search for fairness in the race for life's rewards. As Tyack suggests:

For the most part the workingman did not seek to pull down the rich; rather, they sought equality of opportunity for their children, an equal chance at the main chance. Indeed, in their arguments they appealed, as did the conservatives, to the past: they were only trying to realize "those cardinal principles of republican liberty which were declared in '76, and which can only be sustained by the adoption of an ample system of public instruction, calculated to impart equality as well as mental culture. . . ." When Robert Owen and his followers in New York suggested that all children be taken from their parents and educated in boarding schools where they should have the same food, clothes, and instruction, the workingmen rebelled. They did not want a classless society, nor did they wish to disrupt the basic social institution, the family. Disadvantaged they might be, but they were proud and hoped to better their lot within society as it was.[9]

That is, equality of opportunity in this sense would not lead to equality of outcomes; for it was tacitly recognized that a functioning society required manual laborers, farmers, clerks, and mechanics, as well as lawyers, physicians, managers, and professors. By equality of opportunity was meant "an equal start for all children in the race for life, but their assumption was that some would go farther than others."[10] Differences in ability, effort, luck, and preferences would create differences in outcomes among individuals, but the common school would assure that representative individuals born into any social class would have the same opportunity to achieve status as persons born into other social classes. That is, the opportunities for achieving life success for a son would not be determined by his father's achievements, but only by his own. This major accomplishment would be attained through the common school such that " 'all men are born free and equal'; which equality is preserved until destroyed by the varying degrees of personal merit."[11]

Of note was the fact that equal educational opportunity was considered to be the antecedent for equal opportunity per se. That is, the goal of the common school was equal opportunity and equal educational opportunity represented the means of achieving the goal. Implicit in this policy was the view that, in a just society, the average child from any social origin would begin his adult life with equal chances of success relative to that of a child from another stratum.

It is now clear, in retrospect, that the schools have not achieved this goal. Occupational success, scholastic achievement, and educational attainment of children are still positively correlated with those of parents, although the correlations might have been even higher in the absence of universal schooling.[12] The children of the poor will experience lower incomes, poorer housing, lower occupational status, substandard medical care, and other deficiencies relative to children born into higher socioeconomic strata. The failure of the common school to achieve the social mobility dream must surely raise questions about the role of schooling in achieving equality. Is the job too great for the schools to achieve or is the failure due to a lack of a social structure and commitment that would enable us to truly equalize life's chances for the children of our society?[13]

Human Capital Embodiment

One way of answering that question is to analyze the nature of the task with regard to its implications for educational policy. A useful method of doing this is to view the problem in the context of human capital formation. The concept of human capital has enabled the economist to study how investments in health, education, and training of people lead to increasing productivity and welfare. In essence, the productivity of a population can be related to its human capital embodiment, which is in turn determined by investments in housing, health, nutrition, education, training, and so on.[14] When translated into monetary terms such as increased labor productivity, it appears that the return on investment in human capital often exceeds the return on physical capital (buildings, equipment, etc.).[15]

Let us assume a world in which the opportunities of a particular group of persons are determined solely by the amount of human capital which they possess. That is, we presume that there exists no discrimination in either labor or consumer markets, so that opportunities are determined only by capabilities reflected in human capital embodiment. In such a world, those populations with less human capital would always achieve less lifetime success than those with larger endowments. Indeed, that is the plight faced by children born into disadvantaged families, for by reason of birth alone their families will be able to invest less in them than will their counterparts in more advantaged circumstances.

Families from low socioeconomic origins have a much lesser ability to invest in their offspring in a large variety of areas that affect child development. Before birth, the lower-social-class child is more likely to face prenatal malnutrition.[16] It appears that such nutritional deficiencies may stunt the development of the brain and learning ability.[17] He is less likely to receive adequate medical and dental care as well, so he is more prone to suffer from a large variety of undetected, undiagnosed, and untreated health problems.

The meager income levels associated with lower socioeconomic families translate into less-adequate housing services as they affect child development. Substandard housing exacerbates health problems through inadequate plumbing, increased probability of fires, and other accidents, deficient protection from the elements, and a higher probability of rodents and vermin. As expected, substandard housing tends to be concentrated heavily among the poor and nonwhite.[18] Moreover, children need space and privacy to grow and develop skills that require thought and concentration. The Census Bureau assumes that more than one person per room represents an overcrowded condition, and in 1960 there were about 4 million households living in *standard* units that were overcrowded. For the population as a whole, "three out of ten nonwhite households were crowded in 1960, and one out of ten white households."[19] Research suggests that housing characteristics bear a direct relationship to both the health and productivity of their occupants.[20]

Special Role of the Family

In addition to deficiencies in nutrition, medical services, and shelter, families from lower socioeconomic backgrounds are less able to provide other material inputs which increase human capital. For example, limited family income inhibits or precludes travel and exposure to the large variety of worldly experiences that increase the knowledge and sophistication of the more advantaged child. Perhaps even more important, both the quality and the quantity of parental services as they affect human capital embodiment and future productivity tend to be lower for the disadvantaged child.

Such children are more likely to receive limited parental attention because they are frequently situated in families with many children and where one or both parents are missing.[21] Moreover, in nonwhite families, the mother is more likely to have a job in order to augment the inadequate family income.[22] Further, the lower educational levels of the parents themselves limit the amount of knowledge that they can transmit to their children.[23] While this is a particular drawback in the area of verbal skill development, it is also an inhibiting factor in the embodiment of the more general psychosocial behavior which is required for participation in existing social institutions.[24] The result is that parents with greater educational attainment themselves inculcate in their children much higher skill levels than do parents with less education.[25]

Implications for Financing Equal Educational Opportunity

In summary, if we use the human capital paradigm for diagnosing the problem of moving toward equal opportunity, we can draw the following inferences:

1. To put children born into different social classes on the same starting line for life's rewards will require equal capital embodiment among such groups of persons at the time that they have attained adulthood. This criterion assumes the absence of discrimination against persons from disadvantaged backgrounds. To overcome the obstacles of discrimination may require greater capital embodiment in the children drawn from lower social strata and racial minorities.

2. Differences in capital embodiment among populations stem from many sources, including housing, health services, nutrition, and family investment in educational services and experiences.

3. There is every indication that the differences in capital embodiment when valued in monetary terms are massive, and equalization will require both a heavy social commitment and prodigious public expenditures.

If equal opportunity depends upon equal capital embodiment, then the very circumstances into which the disadvantaged child is born will mean a lower level of investment, capital embodiment, and opportunity for him than for his more advantaged counterpart. Only government intervention is capable of reducing this inequality, since the family and other private sources of investment will always tend to reinforce the disproportionately higher capital embodiment in middle- and upper-class children.

The common school reformers believed that universal public schooling alone could equalize opportunity, partly because they tacitly underestimated the extent of capital embodiment disparities and partly because they had an enormous amount of faith in the efficacy of formal schooling.[26] Indeed, in the mid-nineteenth century, it was probably quite reasonable to believe that equal schooling would give everyone the same chances. First, it was obvious in those days that persons with the highest educations shared the most enviable positions in government and enterprise, so education appeared to be the great path to mobility. Second, the concept of the common school, where children of the rich and poor would sit side by side receiving the same indoctrination conjured images of unprecedented equality. This was particularly poignant in contrast with the elitist educational institutions and social structures of Europe. Taken together, the expectation was that the then revolutionary concept of universal common schooling in a unique society like America could equalize opportunity for all of its citizens.[27]

But, given the assumptions of the capital embodiment model, even equal schooling between children drawn from different social classes will not equalize proficiencies and opportunities. Rather, adding the same educational investment to each group will merely sustain the absolute differences in human capital. Clearly, to equalize capital embodiment will require far greater public investments in the disadvantaged than in the advantaged child if the "opportunity gap" is to be closed. Not only does the child from a disadvantaged background begin school with lower capital embodiment, but he receives less in terms of nonschooling investments even while attending schools. If educational investment is going to narrow the gap, it follows that more must be spent on the education of the disadvantaged child than the advantaged one. How much more depends upon the effectiveness of educational investment in increasing the productive capital of the disadvantaged as well as the urgency with which equality is desired.

Aspects of a Plan for Financing Equal Educational Opportunity

The construction of a plan for financing equal educational opportunity is faced with a myriad of difficulties. Although the previous section outlined a criterion for assessing equality, it is not an easily measurable one. Moreover, the traditional concepts of schooling might not yield easily to necessary changes given that they protect many powerful vested interests. Yet, it is possible to set out certain principles that can be operationalized in such a way as to improve the probability of equal outcome (even if not fully attaining it). Bowles takes a more pessimistic view.[28]

Commitment to Equality

Before proceeding, it is important to note one other obstacle to creating a fairer system of educational finance. It is not clear that there exists a powerful commitment to equality in the manner that we have outlined in the previous section.[29] To achieve equal educational opportunity in this sense will require a transfer of wealth (taxes) from the richer and more powerful to the poorer and weaker segments of the population. Any legislator who votes in favor of such a plan is voting in favor of reducing the lead in the race for life's rewards for children from the upper classes. To add insult to injury, the middle-class parent would be expected to pay to decrease his own child's life chances while enhancing those of the child from lower origins. Yet, consider that the political support for most legislators comes from lobbyists who represent interests of middle- and upper-class America as well as voters whose financial contributions, political participation, and ballots are heavily weighted in favor of richer constituents.

If the first rule of politics is self-survival, then few legislators will show the altruism to increase taxes for the middle and upper classes to effect a salutary improvement in the life conditions of the lower classes. This is not to say that minimal social welfare programs will not be supported, for this society has developed a clear commitment to ensuring a bureaucratic-type subsistence for the poor. But such subsistence programs represent insurance against civil disruption much more than serious attempts at equalizing opportunities. Public welfare programs allow life to proceed for the poor in a dreary, underhoused, underfed, undignified, publicly spied upon, and routinized way, but they do not promote social mobility or self-reliance.[30]

Unfortunately, even among the many legislators who espouse egalitarian goals, a personal commitment to this philosophy is not tantamount to a political commitment. The realities of political life force many public representatives to compromise their consciences at the roll call. Nevertheless, one can still ask what criteria might be used to finance equal educational opportunity if that millennium were to arrive. Accordingly, the remainder of this paper will outline those guidelines by discussing the necessary composition of compensatory education programs, the size of the compensatory investment, the definition of "disadvantaged," and a heuristic application.

Composition of Compensatory Educational Investment

Capital embodiment in a population is defined as the sum of investments from a variety of origins that determine that group's productive capabilities. Sources of such investment include parental interactions, nutrition, health, shelter, and formal education among others. That the disadvantaged share less of these inputs over their lives than the advantaged is a prime cause of inequality of opportunity. Thus, the goal of society would appear to be to equalize average capital embodiment in some sense between the advantaged and the disadvantaged.

If increased educational investment in the disadvantaged is the policy instrument by which this is to be achieved, there exists a basic contradiction in defining the nature of that educational investment. Assume a capital embodiment function,

$$K_{it} = f[M_{i(t)}, D_{i(t)}, N_{i(t)}, S_{i(t)}, F_{i(t)}, I_{i(t)}] \qquad [1]$$

Let K_{it} represent the total capital embodied in the ith population at time t; $M_{i(t)}$ represents the cumulative investment up to time t for medical services; $D_{i(t)}$ signifies the cumulative investment to time t for dental services; $N_{i(t)}$ denotes a comparable measure for nutritional inputs; $S_{i(t)}$ represents the inputs from shelter; $F_{i(t)}$ signifies the cumulative inputs to time t from family interactions and experiences; and $I_{i(t)}$ represents the cumulative effect of the formal instructional services of the school.

In order to understand the nature of educational investment, it is necessary to delineate the relations among these variables in obtaining capital embodiment. Since capital embodiment is defined as the total investment in a population that enables that group to pursue productive opportunities (jobs, income, political power, and so on), it is important to note that not all investment is productive in this sense. For example, beyond certain nutritional requirements, additional dietary inputs do not contribute to the productivity of the individual. Rather, they are eliminated from the body or stored in the fatty tissues, and an excess of alimentary inputs over actual needs for growth and maintenance will be wasted (or even injurious). This is likely to be true of all of the sources of input into capital embodiment function. That is, it is probable that the law of diminishing marginal returns is applicable to the investment function such that concentration on any single source of investment will be wasteful or at least less optimal than dividing investment over all of the requisite inputs.

A second assumed property of [1] is that the effect of any additional input through one source of investment will probably depend upon the levels of investment from other sources. For example, a child with inadequate nutrition or medical care (e.g., untreated vision problems) will likely have a much greater difficulty in learning for any level of instructional inputs than a child who has received higher levels of investment in N and M.

Both these properties suggest that, if equality must be brought about through educational policy alone, then educational services must include far more than instructional services.[31] To a certain degree, the various investment sources might represent substitutes for each other in producing capital embodiment. For example, good instructional services may be able to compensate for many of the educational inputs that the family would normally provide. Yet, as we noted in a previous example, instructional services are probably not substitutable for a protein or vitamin B deficiency, a need for eyeglasses, or a debilitating systemic infection. Accordingly, the compensatory educational budget must be allocated among a variety of investment inputs to obtain a substantial increase in productive capital embodiment of the disadvantaged.

Certainly, the schools have made nominal efforts in these directions with their provision of minimal dental services, free or low-cost milk programs, school lunches, and so on. Both Title I of the Elementary and Secondary Education Act of 1965 and Head Start emphasized that the provision of such "life support" services were legitimate educational inputs.[32] Yet, their importance has been understated in the actual world of expenditures, where the lion's share of so-called compensatory monies is allocated to reduced class sizes and for remedial reading and other instructional specialties.

In the view of this researcher, a much greater portion of investment for equalizing the opportunity for the disadvantaged must take the noninstructional route. More specifically, the following areas of investment are suggestive.

1. A full range of medical and dental services must be considered for children from families who have been excluded from the privileged world of regular and competent diagnosis and treatment. Emphasis should be not only on remedial aspects of health, but also on preventive ones.

2. The role of the schools in providing adequate nutrition should be explored. School breakfasts, as well as free dietary supplements, might represent ways in which the educational system could aid nutrition.

3. Alternatives to private provision of shelter are difficult to suggest. Clearly, study space and room for other activities might be provided for students from substandard and overcrowded housing. Personal development often requires privacy, conditions that may be physically impossible to attain in the existing housing of students from disadvantaged backgrounds.

4. Family inputs can be enhanced through greater school-community involvement. Some methods of doing this include the use of the school for community activities and as a community center as well as the initiation of programs that require parental input, such as tutoring. A greater policy-making role for the community is also a possible approach to increasing family inputs.[33]

5. Instructional inputs have been the traditional area in which school strategies have been implemented. Unfortunately, the specific approaches that have been adopted have often been unimaginative, with heaviest emphasis on increasing personnel within existing programs rather than altering the very programs that have most often been characterized by failure.[34]

More attention must be devoted to alternative instructional approaches if the efficacy of instructional expenditures is to rise.

Thus, equalizing investment for the disadvantaged requires a broad array of programs, not just instructional ones. Unless instructional inputs are completely substitutable for nutritional, health, and other inputs in contributing to the physical, cognitive, and emotional development of youngsters, it will not be possible to achieve equality of opportunity through instructional programs alone. Moreover, even if it were technically possible to substitute heavy doses of instruction for health and other deficiencies, it is likely to represent a very costly strategy relative to a more balanced approach. This can be illustrated by [2] and [3]. The former represents a budget for achieving equality of opportunity.

$$B_{it} = P_1 M_t + P_2 D_t + P_3 N_t + P_4 S_t + P_5 F_t + P_6 I_t \qquad [2]$$

B_{it} represents the budget during the period t for increasing the capital embodiment of the ith population, and $(P_1, P_2, \ldots, P_6)$ represent the unit costs for each additional input of medical services, dental services, nutritional services, shelter, family services, and instructional services, respectively.

Assume that we wish to minimize the budget required to obtain a particular level of capital embodiment during the next period $K_{i(t+1)}$ for the disadvantaged population. Given a choice of the various types of investments in the capital embodiment function 1 and their relative costs $(P_1, \ldots, P_6)$, we wish to determine the minimum budget (total cost) necessary to reach $K_{i(t+1)}$. The standard cost-minimization model would lead to the investment guideline represented by [3], where total investment would be allocated among all inputs until their ratios of marginal products of capital embodiment relative to cost per unit of input were equal for

$$\frac{\partial K_i / \partial M}{P_i} = \frac{\partial K_i / \partial D}{P_2} = \ldots = \frac{\partial K_i / \partial I}{P_6} \qquad [3]$$

all inputs. Now, if all investment were limited to instructional inputs, [3] would be violated, as in [4].

$$\frac{\partial K_i / \partial M}{P_i} = \frac{\partial K_i / \partial D}{P_2} = \ldots > \frac{\partial K_i / \partial I}{P_6} \qquad [4]$$

In the case of [4], the overinvestment in instruction has yielded a smaller contribution to capital embodiment than other alternative investments. Thus, a larger total budget is required than if resources were allocated among all inputs according to their additional productivities. This is the case where an expenditure on eyeglasses or nutritious breakfasts represents a less costly way of increasing student proficiencies than reductions in class size or than alternative instructional approaches. Even if such narrow indicators of capital embodiment as reading scores are used, there is *no* evidence to suggest that instructional investments are more effective relative to their costs than other strategies.[35]

The Magnitude of Differential Investment

The logic of greater educational expenditures on the disadvantaged is straightforward, but the magnitude of the differential must depend on a number of factors. These factors include the relative efficacy of educational investment for achieving equality, the priority for achieving equality, and institutional constraints on expenditure policy.

One way of determining the relative efficacy of educational investment for achieving equality is to think of minimum and maximum values between which there is a range of equalizing effects. That is, let us assume that average educational expenditures on nondisadvantaged children can be represented by E, and we wish to spend more than E for disadvantaged ones. Since the differential in expenditures between the two groups can be characterized by its relationship to E, we can conceive of the ratio d, which denotes the additional multiple of E that is applied to educational spending on disadvantaged students. Thus, per-pupil expenditures on each group can be characterized by E for advantaged students and $(E + dE)$ for disadvantaged ones. If $d = 1$, then spending on the disadvantaged would be twice that on the advantaged; a value of $d = .5$ denotes a 50 percent differential, and so on.[36]

What should be the minimum and maximum values for d? The minimum value should be set at the threshold level, where differential expenditures bring about differential effects. Since the advantaged student continues to receive higher levels of capital investment from his family and other sources during the school period, a minimum differential is needed simply to compensate for ongoing differences in out-of-school influences.[37] Thus, a minimum effort might be needed in order to obtain any effect. The maximum possible value would depend on that point at which additional expenditures yielded no additional increment to human capital. That is, at some point a saturation level is reached, so that additional spending during that period will have no effect on increasing human capital among the disadvantaged relative to that of the advantaged.

Figure 3-1 shows the illustrative minima and maxima for differential educational expenditures in favor of the disadvantaged under

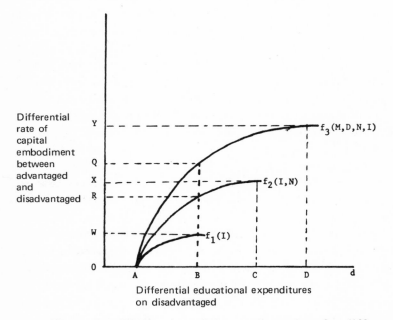

Figure 3-1. Illustrative minima and maxima for differential educational expenditures on the disadvantaged

three sets of investment decisions. The schedule represented by $f_1(I)$ assumes that investment can be channeled to the disadvantaged only through instructional approaches; $f_2(I, N)$ signifies the hypothetical investment relationship when nutritional and instructional approaches are used; and $f_3(M, D, N, I)$ denotes the differential investment effect when medical, dental, nutritional, and instructional services are combined in compensatory programs.

In this illustration, a minimum differential of A is required in order to obtain a threshold difference in the rate of capital embodiment between the advantaged and disadvantaged. That is, A represents the minimum value for d at which educational investment differences in favor of the disadvantaged will increase human capital at a faster rate for the disadvantaged than for the advantaged.

While the minimum differential is shown as being invariant in this illustration, the maximum is dependent on the nature of the investment. The saturation point where additional investment fails to contribute to differential capital embodiment is at B for instructional approaches alone, at C for instruction and nutrition combined, and at D for medical, dental, nutritional, and instructional services combined. That is, the maximum differential is an increasing function of the range of services included in the compensatory investment. When the instructional route alone is selected, the saturation point is reached quickly, while, when investment is distributed across a wider range of services, the potential maximum differential for addressing the equalization of capital embodiment between the two populations is much higher.

A second characteristic of Figure 3-1 is that the rate of equalization per amount of differential investment is an increasing function of the range of services offered. At the saturation point for instructional services alone, B, the rate of equalization is W; but if the same differential $(d=B)$ were applied to instruction and nutritional services, a rate of equalization R would be attained; and if the wider range of services reflected by f_3 were utilized, the rate of equalization of capital embodiment would be higher yet at Q. This phenomenon is reflected by [3] and [4], suggesting that the larger the range of compensatory services offered, the greater the impact of differential expenditures.

Yet, minimum and maximum differentials yield only the technically feasible values that might be applied to compensatory spending. The actual level selected depends not only on this information, but also on the relative priority that the society places on equal opportunity. In the past, the value of d has been negative, a fact which does little to support the view that a large value for d would be feasible politically. That is, traditionally the states have spent greater amounts on the schooling of advantaged students than disadvantaged ones.[38] The larger the value of d—up to the technically feasible maximum—the faster the rate of progress toward equal capital embodiment among populations. Given the large divergencies in capital embodiment that exist at present, even maximum values may mean a time-path to equality that must be measured in centuries. Neither the available technology nor the apparent priorities suggests any rapid movement toward equal capital embodiment.

Defining the Population of Disadvantaged

One of the difficulties in assigning expenditure levels for the education of different groups is that the population does not divide neatly into population groupings of advantaged and disadvantaged. That is, the spectrum of human capital embodiment operates along a hierarchy just as the associated distribution of family wealth and income. Since wealth and income are distributed among the population along a continuous path from abject poverty to fabulous wealth, with the majority of the population between these two poles, it is not an easy task to set out who is disadvantaged by simply drawing a poverty line. When such a device is used to delineate a population, one is confronted with the absurdity that a very small difference in income (or wealth) can transfer a family from poverty status to a nonpoverty one and vice versa. For example, if all families with less than $3,000 are declared to be in poverty, then a family with $2,999 in income is considered to be destitute while one earning $3,001 is not. Yet, for practical purposes, both families are equally poor.

In an excellent analysis of education and poverty, Ribich[39] has outlined a conceptual method for handling this difficulty. Children from families in the lowest income stratum can be considered fully disadvantaged and deserving of a full measure of compensatory expenditure. Students drawn from the lower-middle-income stratum are considered partially disadvantaged with a need for a smaller amount of compensatory spending. Finally, pupils from families at the middle of the income distribution or above are not considered disadvantaged. Thus, they would receive no compensatory monies.

Figure 3-2 illustrates the simplest way of weighing the differential. The horizontal axis shows family income, and the vertical one shows the weight that we will apply to each income class when computing the compensatory differential per student. If we assume that students from families below $3,000 in annual income are fully disadvantaged and those drawn from families with over $9,000 in annual

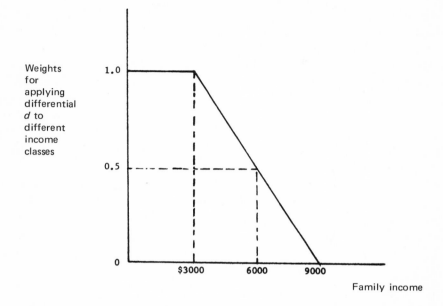

Figure 3-2. Weights for the compensatory spending differential

income are not disadvantaged at all, the respective weights for these two extremes are 1.0 and 0. That is, students from the lower-income category would receive a compensatory expenditure equal to (1.0) d and those in the higher bracket would receive none (0) d. Students from families between the $3,000-$9,000 limits would benefit by some ratio of d depending upon where they were on the spectrum. In this illustration, students from families with about $4,500 in annual income would benefit by (.75) d; pupils from families with $6,000 would receive (.5) in compensatory spending and so on.

Accordingly, the amount of differential expenditure for equalizing capital embodiment could be calculated simply by knowing the number of students drawn from each income class and the appropriate weights. In this way, it would even be possible to coordinate compensatory spending with the state income tax. All households would be required to file a tax return, even if they received no income during the year. Based upon the family income, number of children in the family, and perhaps other criteria, the State Division of Taxation would report to the State Department of Education, the school district in which the family was enrolled, and the eligible family what the compensatory differential would be for the next year. Thus, no local means test would be required. On the basis of the April 15 deadline for filing tax returns, the State Department of Education, school districts, and families could know by May 15 the amount of differential spending that students and schools would be eligible to receive.[40]

Indeed, it is possible that the differential could be allocated to each family in the form of a voucher that was applicable to the purchase of approved services, whether instructional, medical, dental, nutritional, and so on.[41] Moreover, the treatment of the differential on a family-by-family basis will improve the accountability of compensatory expenditures. Past practices of some school districts have led to such monies being used for the education of students other than those who were eligible under the law.[42]

A Heuristic Approach to Financing Education

One way of suggesting how to implement some of the concepts that were described in the foregoing analysis is to suggest a general approach for allocating the state educational budget. The total expenditure for the ith school district might be represented by [5].

$$T_i = EN_i + aN_i + C_i + D_i + dE \sum_{j=1}^{n} W_i N_{ji} \qquad [5]$$

T_i is the total expenditure for the ith district, E denotes the basic per pupil expenditure that applies to the student membership of the district N_i; a represents a cost differential that is applicable only to those districts where labor, land, and other costs are higher than normal; C_i denotes a flat sum allocable to the district by the state for mandated transportation; D_i is a flat sum allotted to the district according to the state formula for educating exceptional children and similar tasks; d is the differential ratio of E for equalizing opportunity; W_j is the weight for the jth income class; and N_{ji} represents the number of pupils drawn from the jth income class.

If the state were to assume all the costs of education, it might allocate all monies in [5] directly to school districts except for the last element, the compensatory education portion. This amount might be allotted directly to parents in the form of a voucher as described previously. Families might be given the choice of a large variety of compensatory services both within and outside the school.

Moreover, even if part of the voucher were applied to narrow instructional services such as reading, the student and his family might be able to select alternatives to the public schools for this function. That is, private firms and other groups would be certified to compete for student vouchers.

In such a case, accountability would be established by requiring that all approved firms or groups must record the progress of each child and supply such information to the child's parents, the school, and the state accrediting agency; moreover, differential success of firms would also be published at stated intervals, perhaps annually or biannually. Under this arrangement, the public schools would also be eligible to receive vouchers, providing that they fulfilled the accountability requirements of the state. Children could be released from part of the standard curriculum to receive such specialized services.

The logic underlying this plan is based upon the fact that the schools have shown their greatest failures in adapting to the individualized needs of their students. Even the approaches made toward compensatory education have emphasized a curriculum or a technique for all of the so-called disadvantaged students in the school or even in the school system. It would seem that the market approach would work best for specialized educational needs in the sense that the firms could concentrate on fairly narrow objectives, while allowing the schools to concentrate on the broader aspects of education, especially those that require a close tie to the general needs of the community.

Notes

This paper was prepared for a special issue of *Education and Urban Society*, published in February 1973, and addressed to educational financing in light of *Serrano* v. *Priest*. The author has drawn heavily upon his reports to the New York State Commission on the Quality, Cost and Financing of Elementary and Secondary Education.

1. *Serrano* v. *Priest* (1971), 5 Cal. 3d 584,487 P. 2d 1241.

2. See, for example, Citizens Commission of Maryland Government, "A Responsible Plan for the Financing, Governance, and Evaluation of Maryland's Public Schools," (Baltimore, 1971); New York State Commission on the Quality, Cost and Financing of Elementary and Secondary Education, *Report* (New York, 1972).

3. F. V. Fowlkes, "Economics Report—Administration Leans to Value-added Tax to Help Solve National Fiscal Crises," *National Journal* (February 5, 1972), 210-19.

4. *Harvard Educational Review* 38 (Winter 1968).

5. Lester C. Thurow, *Poverty and Discrimination* (Washington, D.C.: Brookings Institution, 1969); G. Hanoch, "An Economic Analysis of Earnings and Schooling," *Journal of Human Resources* 2 (Summer 1967), 310-29; Samuel Bowles, "Schooling and Inequality from Generation to Generation," *Journal of Political Economy* 80 (May-June 1972), S219-51; Z. Griliches and W. M. Mason, "Education, Income, and Ability," *Journal of Political Economy* 80 (May-June 1972), S74-103.

6. Samuel Bowles, "Unequal Education and the Reproduction of the Social Division of Labor," in Martin Carnoy (ed.) *Schooling in a Corporate Society* (New York: David McKay, 1972), 36-66.

7. That is, even in an "unfair" society, an improvement in one part of the system is still preferable to no improvement at all.

8. Horace Mann, *The Republic and the School* (New York: Columbia University Teachers College, 1957).

9. David B. Tyack, *Turning Points in American Educational History* (Waltham, Mass.: Blaisdell, 1967).

10. Arthur Mann, "A Historical Overview: The *Lumpenproletariat*, Education, and Compensatory Action," in Charles U. Daly (ed.) *The Quality of Inequality: Urban and Suburban Public Schools* (Chicago: University of Chicago Press, 1968), 9-26.

11. Mann, *op. cit.*; E. Abbott and S. P. Breckenridge, *Truancy and Non-attendance in the Chicago Schools* (Chicago: Arno, 1971).

12. For research on these relationships, see Griliches and Mason, *op. cit.*; Bowles, "Schooling and Inequality from Generation to Generation"; O. D. Duncan, *Socioeconomic Background and Occupational Achievement Extensions of a Basic Model* (Washington, D.C.: U.S. Department of Health, Education and Welfare, 1968).

13. This question is raised in H. M. Levin, "Social Utility, Equal Educational Opportunity, and Educational Investment Policy," Report to the New York State Commission on the Quality, Cost and Financing of Elementary and Secondary Education, Part 2 (July 1971).

14. T. W. Schultz, "The Human Capital Approach to Education," in R. L. Johns *et al.*, *Economic Factors Affecting the Financing of Education* (Gainesville, Fla.: National Educational Finance Project, 1970), ch. 2; G. S. Becker, *Human Capital* (New York: Columbia University Press, 1964).

15. T. W. Schultz, "The Rate of Return in Allocating Investment Resources to Education," *Journal of Human Resources* 2 (Summer 1967), 293-309.

16. U. S. Department of Health, Education, and Welfare, *Perspectives on Human Deprivation: Biological, Psychological and Sociological* (Washington, D.C.: Public Health Service, 1968); A. D. Berg, "Nutrition as a National Priority: Lessons from the India Experiment," *American Journal of Clinical Nutrition* 23 (November 1970), 1396-1408.

17. N. S. Scrimshaw and J. E. Gordon (eds.), *Malnutrition, Learning and Behavior* (Cambridge, Mass.: MIT Press, 1968).

18. President's Committee on Urban Housing, *A Decent Home* (Washington, D.C.: U.S. Government Printing Office, 1968).

19. *Ibid.*

20. R. G. Healy, "Effects of Improved Housing on Worker Performance," *Journal of Human Resources* 2 (Summer 1971), 297-309.

21. U. S. Department of Labor, *The Negro Family: The Case for National Action* (Washington, D.C.; Government Printing Office, 1965); for trend data, see R. Farley, "Family Types and Family Headship: A Comparison of Trends among Blacks and Whites," *Journal of Human Resources* 6 (Summer 1971), 297-309.

22. According to the Department of Labor survey taken in March 1966, 47.17 percent of nonwhite mothers with children under the age of eighteen were in the labor force, while the comparable figure for whites was 34.3 percent. U.S. Department of Labor, *Wage and Labor Standards, Negro Women in the Population and in the Labor Force* (Washington, D.C.: Government Printing Office, 1967).

23. Ellis G. Olim, Robert D. Hess, and Virginia Shipman, "The Role of Mothers' Language Styles in Mediating Their Preschool Children's Cognitive Development," *School Review* 75 (Winter 1967), 414; Robert D. Hess, Virginia Shipman, and D. Jackson, "Early Experience and the Socialization of Cognitive Modes in Children," *Child Development* 36 (December 1965), 869-86.

24. For an excellent review, see U. S. Department of Health, Education and Welfare, *Perspectives on Human Deprivation: Biological, Psychological and Sociological,* chs. 1, 2.

25. The association of parental education and socioeconomic status with children's scholastic performance is probably the most consistent finding in studies of academic achievement. See J. S. Coleman *et al., Equality of Educational Opportunity* (Washington, D.C.: Government Printing Office, 1966).

26. L. A. Cremin, *The American Common School: An Historic Conception* (New York: Bureau of Publications, Teachers College, Columbia University, 1951), chs. 1, 2.

27. For a general social and political comparison of the United States and Europe in the 1830's, see A. de Tocqueville, *Democracy in America* (New York: Alfred A. Knopf, 1946).

28. For a more pessimistic view, see Bowles, "Schooling and Inequality from Generation to Generation."

29. H. M. Levin, "Social Utility, Equal Educational Opportunity, and Educational Investment Policy."

30. F. F. Piven and R. A. Cloward, *Regulating the Poor: The Function of Public Welfare* (New York: Pantheon, 1971); I. Kristol, "Welfare: The Best of Intentions, the Worst of Results," *Atlantic* 228 (August 1971), 45-47.

31. The assertion that noninstructional services are provided at adequate levels by other agencies is not supported by fact. See, for example, the reports issued by the Select Committee on Nutrition and Human Needs of the U.S. Senate in August and September of 1969 and in January of 1971.

32. For example, of almost $700 million of Title I allocations spent during the regular school year of 1967-68, about $26 million was allotted to food services and $19 million to health services. See U. S. Department of Health, Education, and Welfare, *Statistical Report Fiscal Year 1968: A Report on*

the Third Year of Title I ESEA, OE-37021-68 (Washington, D.C.: U.S. Office of Education, 1970)

33. H. M. Levin (ed.), *Community Control of Schools* (Washington, D.C.: Brookings Institution, 1970).

34. For a panoramic view, see A. Stein, "Strategies for Failure," *Harvard Educational Review* 41 (May 1971), 158-204.

35. In fact, one of the reasons that instructional remedies have shown such poor results may stem from the interdependence between other types of student well-being and academic performance.

36. In the context of the model outlined in H. M. Levin, "Social Utility, Equal Educational Opportunity, and Educational Investment Policy," it is obvious that $d = P_2/P_1 - 1$.

37. For example, Dugan estimated that the market value of the flow of mother's educational services to the child between grades 1 and 12 was only $3,000 for a student whose mother was a grade school graduate, but over $8,000 for a student whose mother graduated from college. D. Dugan, "The Impact of Parental and Educational Investment upon Student Achievement," paper presented at the annual meeting of the American Statistical Association, New York City, August 21, 1969.

38. J. E. Coons, W. H. Clune, III, and S. D. Sugarman, *Private Wealth and Public Education* (Cambridge, Mass.: Belknap Press, 1970); J. W. Guthrie, G. B. Kleindorfer, H. M. Levin, and R. T. Stout, *Schools and Inequality* (Cambridge, Mass.: MIT Press, 1971).

39. T. I. Ribich, *Education and Poverty* (Washington, D.C.: Brookings Institution, 1968), ch. 2.

40. Income averaging for a three- to five-year period might be used as the basis for computing eligibility. In this way, temporary fluctuations in family income would not create spurious fluctuations from year to year in student expenditure. Family size and other relevant characteristics might be used to calculate the amount of the educational differential.

41. For readings on vouchers, see Milton Friedman, *Capitalism and Freedom* (Chicago: University of Chicago Press, 1962), ch. 6; Center for the Study of Public Policy, *Education Vouchers: A Report on Financing Elementary Education by Grants to Parents* (Cambridge, Mass.: Center for the Study of Public Policy, 1970); H. M. Levin, "The Failure of Schools and the Free Market Remedy," *Urban Review* 2 (June 1968), 32-37.

42. R. Martin and P. McClure, *Title I of ESEA: Is It Helping Poor Children?* (Washington, D.C.: Washington Research Project and NAACP Legal Defense and Educational Fund, 1969).

4. Assimilation, Pluralism, and Separatism in American Education

Edgar G. Epps

The proper role of the schools in the socialization of Afro-American, Mexican-American, Native American, Asian-American, European-American, and mainland Puerto Rican children is a matter of great concern to social scientists, educators, and policy makers. Schools have simultaneously served both assimilative and discriminative functions in American society. Both the assimilative and discriminative forces are apparent in the monocultural curriculum of the schools and the systematic relationship between schooling and social mobility. The assimilative force has made it possible for the children of Poles, Germans, Swedes, Italians, and Irishmen to blend with descendants of earlier European immigrants. On the other hand, the discriminative force has made it extremely difficult for the children of recent immigrants and racial minorities to acquire the quality and quantity of education required for successful competition in the occupational system of an urbanized technological society.

Traditionally, American society has been willing to accept culturally different peoples if they were willing to become acculturated and reject their cultural distinctiveness. At the same time, the American social system has maintained economic, educational, political, and legal systems which discriminate against those who are culturally

This paper is a revised and expanded version of "Education for Black Americans: Outlook for the Future," which originally appeared in *School Review* 81 (May 1973). Used with permission of the University of Chicago Press.

49

or physically different. A special burden is placed upon members of groups with observable badges of discrimination: pigmentation, physical features, and accent. The discrimination includes aspects of ethnic, class, and racial chauvinism.

Schools cannot be isolated from the society that created them. "Thus when there are problems in the schools . . . one should look in the larger society for their source. And since bad schools . . . reflect the malaise of their surrounding environment, they can only be 'cured' when the collective life of the community is strengthened."[1] The definition of the function of the schools, formed during the period from 1830 to 1880, is based on an ethnocentric philosophy dedicated to the remodeling of citizens to conform to a single homogeneous model of acceptable behavior. The result is a system of public education that is class biased and racist. Schools, therefore, serve two broad societal functions: they Americanize (homogenize) students, and they sort, filter, and accredit children of diverse backgrounds into sex, class, and racial-ethnic roles. *"Implicitly and explicitly, students are taught that Western culture is a male-oriented, white-based enterprise."*[2]

The present educational situation in which schools fail to educate large numbers of blacks and other minority lower-class children to even the minimal level expected of American adults is one manifestation of the price of being nonwhite, non-Anglo-European, and non-middle class in America. The combination of a belief in the intellectual inferiority of lower-class children and minority-group children and the need for a large pool of low-paid, unskilled labor has resulted in educational policies that operate to keep low-status groups at the bottom of the occupational structure while maintaining the favored position of high-status groups. Policy makers tout education as the pathway to success and participation in the mainstream of society while at the same time they design programs which relegate subordinate groups to low-status positions and lives of poverty.

In spite of the fact that American education has served them so poorly in the past, black Americans share with other ethnic groups the belief that education is the means by which groups move from rejection, poverty, and political exclusion to acceptance, economic sufficiency, and political inclusion. Few Americans today would disagree with the principle of equality of educational opportunity for all racial, religious, and ethnic groups. There is considerable disagreement, however, on the meaning of equal educational opportunity.

Inequality of Opportunity: The Black Experience

The traditional view of equal educational opportunity stresses equal access to schooling. In this view, equality of educational opportunity is attained when there is roughly equal opportunity for different segments of the population to compete for the benefits of the educational system.[3] The modern view of equality goes much further. According to James Coleman, there are at least five ways to conceptualize inequality of opportunity:

first, inequality defined by degree of racial segregation; second, inequality of resource inputs from the school system; third, inequality in "intangible" resources such as teacher morale; fourth, inequality of inputs as weighted according to their effectiveness for achievement; and fifth, inequality of output as prima facie evidence of inequality of opportunity.[4]

Inequality of inputs. The first, second, and third definitions of inequality are concerned with inequality of inputs whether defined in terms of the race and class of one's fellow students or in terms of financial resources, facilities, and personnel. In its desegregation decision of 1954, the Supreme Court held that separate schools for black and white children are inherently unequal. By this yardstick, American public education remains largely unequal in nearly every school system in the United States. Because of its prior history of legal segregation, efforts to eliminate segregated schools have proceeded more rapidly in the South than in the North. However, court decisions in Richmond, Detroit, and other cities may result in desegregation of schools in large urban systems through metropolitan desegregation plans that include contiguous suburban districts. This approach is necessary because recent white migration to the suburbs has resulted in such massive population shifts that many large city systems are predominantly black and may become all-black within the decade. The result of this "white flight" is that resegregation proceeds almost as rapidly as desegregation. Metropolitan desegregation plans would shut off the escape routes.

When inequality is defined in terms of the resource inputs from the school system, we also find inequality both within systems and between inner-city schools and suburban schools. Recently Coleman has pointed out that, even if actual dollar expenditures within a system are disbursed equitably by the board of education, there is still the question of inequality of inputs as *received by the child.*[5]

For example, if a school board spends the same amount for textbooks in two schools with the same number of children but which serve children of different social-class backgrounds, the books may be of lesser value to children in the lower-class school because the content of the books is more attuned to the interests and academic styles of middle-class children. In other words, there may be a loss of input between what is disbursed and what is received which operates to reduce the resources received by the average black child.

When we look at "intangible resources" such as teacher morale, we encounter two problems. On the one hand, schools attended by blacks are considered to be low-status schools from which upwardly mobile teachers seek to escape as fast as possible. On the other hand, blacks are viewed by many teachers and administrators as being difficult pupils. Kenneth B. Clark has placed much of the responsibility for the academic problems of ghetto children squarely on the teachers and school administrators.[6] Negative labels such as "culturally deprived," and "learning disability" may be used as excuses for educational neglect. According to this view, a key factor leading to the academic failure of ghetto children is the fact that generally their teachers do not expect them to learn, and have adopted, as their concept of their function, custodial care and discipline.

Advocates of community control, decentralization, and various separatist alternatives to the public schools base much of their argument on two beliefs. First, they are very doubtful that white-controlled educational systems will distribute material resources equitably. Second, they are even more doubtful about such intangibles as teacher attitudes and expectations. They argue for community control as a means of assuring equitable distribution of both types of inputs.

Inequality of outputs. The fourth definition of inequality raises questions about the effectiveness of inputs for enhancing children's achievement. Equalizing finances, facilities, and other resources may have little effect on children's achievement. More precisely, some inputs may be more important for achievement than others. Unfortunately, there is little reliable information available in this area. Proponents of specialized programs make strong claims for their effectiveness, but none has been shown to be unequivocally superior to others. Proponents of desegregation as an intervention strategy to improve black children's achievement encounter the same problem. The results are mixed and subject to considerable controversy.

While the legal case for desegregation has been spelled out clearly in court decisions, there is considerable controversy as to whether or not children derive educational benefits from desegregation other than those attributable to such inputs as improved curricula, better teachers, and better facilities. There are still very few hard data that would allow us to state unequivocally that, given equal inputs, children would still receive inferior education in all-black schools. It is often contended that racially identifiable schools have harmful effects on the achievement, self-concepts and attitudes of all children. While this view is held by many educators and social psychologists and is supported by the results of the Coleman Report, opposition is now developing on two fronts. The first attack comes from studies of the effects of desegregation which raise questions about the benefits in terms of improved achievement for black children and increased racial tolerance for white children.[7] In spite of the controversy concerning the educational and social benefits of desegregation, there is general agreement that student benefits are greater in biracial situations where conflict and hostility are at a minimum. A distinction is made between "desegregation" and "integration." Congenial racial interaction is typically considered to be a necessary ingredient of an "integrated" situation, while the mere presence of children of different races is sufficient for desegregation. The bulk of the evidence so far suggests that increased racial tolerance and improved achievement occur only in "integrated" situations and that both tolerance and achievement may decline in "desegregated" situations.

The other point of attack is concerned with the implicit racism of a philosophy that assumes that black children can learn effectively only when they are in classrooms where the majority of the students are white. While the proponents of integration do not state their position so bluntly, there is the clear assumption that black schools are inferior although this inferiority is usually explained in terms of differential resources. Black opponents of desegregation may point to research results which indicate that self-esteem and race pride are higher in black schools than in biracial schools.[8] They may also note the paucity of research *with adequate controls for selectivity* among studies purporting to show improved achievement in biracial schools. At least one study reports results indicating that community-controlled schools can enhance academic achievement.[9] Since there are reasons to doubt the effectiveness of desegregation as an intervention strategy that will lead to better-quality education for black children, many people are asking whether or not the hardships associated with desegregation are too great a price to pay for such nebulous returns.

When inequality is defined in terms of benefits or outputs, we are also faced with the problem of deciding what criteria should be used to measure achievement. Typically, achievement test scores are used as criterion measures. In some instances, I.Q. scores have been used for this purpose. Scores on these tests are used to measure gains in achievement within a group or to compare achievement between groups. The worth of a program or the progress of a group is determined by changes in test scores. This practice is widespread in spite of the fact that many questions have been raised about the appropriateness of using tests standardized on whites to assess achievement in groups with different cultural and linguistic backgrounds. The testing issue is extremely important, but it is too complex for inclusion in this paper.[10] At this point, it is sufficient to draw attention to the importance attached to test results while questions of validity are still being debated and knowledge concerning the relationship of group experience and values to cognitive styles and learning patterns is still extremely limited.

In attempting to assess the relative merits of desegregation, integration, decentralization, or various curriculum strategies, the criterion issue is of greatest importance. Certainly black parents want their children to learn to read and to acquire the skills needed for social and occupational success. For some parents, other concerns are equally important. For example, does the school provide an opportunity for the child to learn about his cultural heritage? Is he able to share in the psychological rewards associated with being identified as a member of a group whose contributions to the development of the nation have been important and respected? Does he have an opportunity to acquire a sense of competence, a positive self-image, and a sense of group pride?

For persons who share these concerns, desegregation as currently practiced raises the specter of the elimination of minority group culture. For them, the danger is that school desegregation may result in cultural homogenization. They would prefer to seek solutions that provide opportunities for acquiring the knowledge and technical skills needed to survive in an urbanized technological society without having to become alienated from one's social heritage.

Integration and Community Control

The issue of integration is one of the most controversial dilemmas still facing American educators and politicians. In a recent article, William Taylor provides a good description of the important cases and the key legal issues still before the courts.[11] He states that the crucial elements of the Richmond and Detroit decisions were: (1) state responsibility for public education; (2) the containment of black people in the central city by policies of housing discrimination; and (3) the lack of justification for maintaining separate districts in a single metropolitan community where such districting resulted in segregated schools. He argues that logistic problems involving transportation of children are manageable and may be resolved without undue hardship to children. He also argues that metropolitan desegregation, if accompanied by decentralization, need not decrease opportunities for community participation.

Not all black parents agree that the goal of integration is worth the sacrifices involved, especially when children must bear the burden of racial hostility. In addition to opposition based on concerns about possible negative consequences of metropolitan desegregation for children, some black leaders oppose this strategy because it may lead to metropolitan government. Such a development, they argue, would dilute black voting strength and make it difficult for blacks to elect representatives to local, state, and federal governing bodies. Taylor counters this argument by pointing out that representation is a separate legal issue that must be handled apart from the school issue.

Robert Green also feels that there is no necessary conflict between the goals of community participation and metropolitan desegregation.[12] He argues for a broader definition of community than that commonly used by advocates of community control. He envisions a biracial educational community, based on school attendance districts rather than on geography or ethnicity. Metropolitan desegregation accompanied by decentralization of administrative functions would permit parents to have as much influence in metropolitan school affairs as they currently have in suburban districts. Green, like Taylor, views bussing as a viable mechanism for eliminating segregation in metropolitan districts. No other approach is likely to result in any lasting desegregation. When combined with decentralization, the concept of metropolitan school desegregation could serve the goals of both integration and community control.

Many blacks prefer a more nationalistic concept of community control than that used by Green. Rodney Reed argues that the push for community control of public schools is essentially a political reform movement whose objective is to wrest power from traditional boards of education and shift it to local communities or school districts.[13] There is an assumption that such a shift in power will make schools more responsive to the needs of black children and black communities and decrease alienation between school and community. Reed also states that community control of schools can and should result in improved student academic performance because teachers and administrators would be accountable to the community. This, he asserts, would lead to "a climate of individual respect" and higher pupil expectations which should lead to improved achievement. While there is no evidence that these educational benefits would be forthcoming, there is little doubt that community control would challenge the current urban power blocs as exemplified by the central school boards and teachers unions. Other than increasing the proportion of black teachers and administrators, and the expansion of black-oriented programs and materials, community control advocates have not described in sufficient detail the processes involved in improving the quality of education available to black children. It is probable that if community control became a reality, few black educators would be prepared to implement programs that would lead to improved achievement. It is also probable that there would be considerable disagreement among blacks about appropriate criteria of achievement or what constitutes a good program. The political goals of community control are more clearly defined than the educational goals.

How prevalent are racial solidarity sentiments in black communities? Results of interviews in one northern and one southern city provide an estimate of the extent to which having black teachers for black students, black control of black schools, and using bussing to implement desegregation are endorsed by black adults.[14] Comparing these results with the results of other surveys, the authors conclude that black solidarity sentiments are on the rise. However, about one-fifth of the sample agree that black students should have only black teachers, more than one-third agree that black educators should run black schools, but more than half agree that bussing does more harm than good. These results suggest that there is considerable support for multiracial staffing and administration of schools, but little support for bussing. It is interesting to note that southerners are more in favor of bussing than northerners, and that more highly educated respondents are less likely to endorse community control and all black teachers than less educated respondents, but are more favorable toward bussing. Age and sex also affected responses to these issues, as did degree of alienation as measured by an anomie scale. The authors conclude that pressures for separatist or nationalist solutions to educational problems are more likely to come from lower-status urban blacks than from more advantaged blacks. These results suggest that unless the better-educated segment of the black community increases its support for community control and other nationalistic strategies, the political clout needed to bring about such changes in school organization will not be forthcoming.

One result of the increase in black solidarity sentiment that has taken place in the past few years has been an increase in the number of black school administrators. If community control movements are successful, systems with largely black students are likely to turn increasingly to black administrators in an effort to find the kind of leadership needed to improve educational quality. Charles Moody has described some of the experiences of pioneer black superintendents and the problems they faced.[15] Moody's account makes it clear that hiring a black superintendent is no panacea, especially if the school system is not prepared to provide him with adequate resources and authority to get the job done. Moody's article suggests that black administrators are rarely brought into a system before it has already become financially and politically impossible to manage. The position of black superintendents parallels that of black mayors; typically they are brought into a situation in which local resources are grossly inadequate and where they cannot improve conditions without assistance from state and federal agencies. The end result is a powerless top administrator who takes the blame for educational problems but cannot mobilize the resources needed to improve on the situation. Community control of schools, including the school board and the superintendent, is meaningless without adequate resources and local control of those resources.

Education for Liberation

Barbara Sizemore argues that the most effective programs for the masses of the African-American poor seem to be those which encourage self-determination along cultural-ethno-religious lines.[16] She draws on the work of Carter Woodson as well as the experiences of African leaders to develop a rationale for educational strategies that would lead to self-reliance. According to Sizemore, the heart of the black liberation curriculum is the dialogue which must be carried on with the learner through all the institutions serving him, the school, the church, the family, and the community organization. Such a curriculum uses the language and life style of the learner to facilitate learning. She also suggests that, in situations of powerlessness, it may be more important to develop collective orientations than individual orientations. In order to implement a liberation curriculum in the public schools, community control or decentralization would be necessary. To be effective, however, the local board would have to have veto power on matters of personnel and budget. She concludes that African-Americans must answer the following questions before they can design an educational program for liberation: (1) What kind of person do we want? (2) What kind of society will we build? (3) What will education be designed to do? (4) What kind of program will prepare the masses for liberation within a capitalist framework which guarantees losers? We also need a better understanding of the way the oppressive society operates, and a better understanding of the strengths of the oppressed community which could be mobilized for liberation.

According to James Banks, the ultimate goal of a liberation curriculum is to make black students intelligent political activists so that they will know how to get and maintain power.[17] Banks contends that we must create an open society in America to liberate blacks from oppression. This would require the redistribution of power so that currently excluded groups could share power with dominant groups. It is not clear how this redistribution of power is to come about, but Banks assumes that education can play a role in bringing it to pass if the curriculum is structured properly. This assumption seems to be based on the highly probabilistic eventuality that those in power will not recognize the revolution taking place in the schools and prevent its occurrence.

Higher Education for Black Americans

Whether one takes a nationalistic or an integrationist approach to black education, there is little disagreement among blacks on the need for increasing the numbers and proportions of blacks attaining higher education. The black community needs well-trained leaders and professionals. The Carnegie Commission on Higher Education has estimated that the number of blacks in college should double by the end of this decade and double again by the year 2000. Most of this increase will take place in white colleges and universities because, even at full capacity enrollments, the 100 or so black colleges cannot accommodate more than one-fourth of the anticipated increase in black student enrollment.

There currently are about 520,000 black college students. Of the black students who entered four-year colleges in 1971 approximately 35 percent entered black institutions and about 34 percent entered white institutions.[18] The remaining entering black students enrolled in two-year colleges. It is probable that dropout and completion rates in the two types of four-year institutions will be somewhat comparable, but it is also quite probable that a much smaller proportion of students entering two-year colleges will complete a baccalaureate degree. Since the large increase in black enrollments has taken place quite recently, most of these students are still in the first two years of college. It will be another year or two before we will know with any degree of certainty whether or not the white colleges which, according to Alan Bayer, are attracting the best black students are also providing them with sufficient resources to see them through the matriculation process to graduation. It is of interest to note that students at black colleges are more likely to have graduate school aspirations. Whether this is a result of self-selection, recruitment, or institutional impact is also a question about which we need additional information.

While there is little disagreement about the fact that lower-class, non-Anglo-European Americans are being miseducated today as in the past, there is little consensus as to the most effective way to eliminate such miseducation and replace it with appropriate education.

One type of miseducation is manifested in the failure of American education to do an effective job of preparing lower-class non-Anglo

European children for competition in an urbanized technological society. If one accepts an assimilationist view of American education,
the problem of appropriate education for non-Anglo-European
Americans is perceived as one of making the system work for other
groups in the same manner it works for Anglo-Europeans. This is
essentially a reformist position which looks to such strategies as integration, reorganization of school financing, curriculum revision, and
compensatory education to eradicate inequities in the system. Such
reforms, if successful, would eliminate race and ethnicity as discriminatory factors, but leave intact those aspects of the educational
system which discriminate according to social class. Since non-Anglo-
European families are more likely than Anglo-Europeans to be found
in the lower class, such reforms are not likely to eliminate group
differences in social position.

Another type of miseducation is manifested in the Anglo-Euro-
pean bias that permeates almost all educational theory and practice.
Appropriate education in a pluralistic society would begin with the
development of programs that use the cultural contexts of the populations served by the school to determine the values, goals, and content of education. The focus in some schools may be nationalistic,
even separatist; in others the emphasis may be bicultural; in still
others, multicultural. The objective is to utilize the diversity that
exists in this society to help children learn and to encourage a
healthy respect for cultural differences. Some educators propose a
type of education which would help oppressed peoples develop a
political consciousness and a knowledge of the social structure that
will enable them to attain power and maintain it. Advocates of this
approach do not minimize the need for children to acquire academic
skills; they want the acquisition of skills to occur within a framework
that will encourage ethnic group members to work for political self-
determination and economic development of their own communities.

Two recent historical works seriously question the widely accepted belief that the public schools have served as the primary
source of acculturation and eventual upward social mobility for immigrants and other low-status groups.[19] The authors argue that the
public schools have always operated to preserve the status quo, that
schools have had little impact on the relative positions of ethnic
groups in America, and that blacks and other minorities would be
extremely naïve to place their hopes for equality on the schools.

There is little doubt that the schools have served some groups better than others. The basic question is whether or not the groups benefiting most from the schools were more advantaged upon entry into the system than groups benefiting less from the system. The bulk of the evidence seems to support an affirmative answer. Immigrant groups whose members had relatively high status in their home countries, came from urban settings, or had strong intellectual traditions fared rather well in the schools. Those groups comprised of low-status immigrants, from rural settings, without strong intellectual traditions encountered problems similar to those faced by contemporary minorities. The major difference today is that minority groups are no longer willing to accept this state of affairs as normal or just.

Many writers have approached black education as if there is a homogeneous entity called the black community. It should not be necessary to remind educators and social scientists that blacks in America range from rich to poor, urban to rural, well-educated to illiterate, politically conservative to revolutionary, and from separatist to integrationist. Political leaders, educators, and other policy makers must take this diversity into consideration as they evaluate strategies to bring to an end the miseducation of black Americans.

Notes

1. Sarane S. Boocock, "The School as a Social Environment for Learning: Social Organization and Micro-Social Process in Education," *Sociology of Education* 46 (Winter 1973), 17.

2. Norman Denzin, "Children and Their Caretakers," *Transaction* 8 (July-August 1971), 62-72.

3. Thomas F. Green, "The Dismal Future of Equal Educational Opportunity," in Thomas F. Green (ed.), *Educational Planning in Perspective* (New York: IPC [American], Incorporated, 1971), 27.

4. James S. Coleman, "The Evaluation of *Equality of Educational Opportunity*," in Frederick Mosteller and Daniel P. Moynihan (eds.), *On Equality of Educational Opportunity* (New York: Vintage Press, 1972), 147.

5. *Ibid.*

6. Kenneth B. Clark, *Dark Ghetto* (New York: Harper and Row, 1965).

7. David Armor, "The Evidence on Busing," *The Public Interest* (Summer 1972); Elizabeth Useem, "White Students and Token Desegregation," *Integrated Education* 10 (September-October 1972), 46-54.

8. Bernard Rosenberg and Roberta Simmons, *Black and White Self-Esteem: The Urban School Child* (Washington, D. C.: The American Sociological Association, 1971); and Lafayette Lipscomb, "Racial Identity of Nursery School

Children," paper presented at the annual meeting of the American Sociological Association, New Orleans, Louisiana, August 1972.

9. Marcia Guttentag, "Children in Harlem's Community Controlled Schools," *Journal of Social Issues* 28 (No. 4, 1972), 1-20.

10. See Ralph W. Tyler and Richard M. Wolf (eds.), *Crucial Issues in Testing* (Berkeley, Calif.: McCutchan Publishing Corporation, 1974) for a discussion of issues referred to here.

11. William L. Taylor, "The Legal Battle for Metropolitanism," *School Review* 81 (May 1973), 331-45.

12. Robert L. Green, "Community Control and Desegregation," *ibid.*, 347-56.

13. Rodney J. Reed, "The Community School Board," *ibid.*, 357-63.

14. William J. Wilson, Castellano B. Turner, and William A. Darity, "Racial Solidarity and Separate Education," *ibid.*, 365-73.

15. Charles D. Moody, "The Black Superintendent," *ibid.*, 375-82.

16. Barbara A. Sizemore, "Education for Liberation," *ibid.*, 389-404.

17. James A. Banks, "Curriculum Strategies for Black Liberation," *ibid.*, 405-14.

18. Alan E. Bayer, "The New Student in Black Colleges," *ibid.*, 415-26.

19. Colin Greer, *The Great School Legend: A Revisionist Interpretation of American Public Education* (New York: Basic Books, 1972); Michael Katz, *Class, Bureaucracy, and Schools: The Illusion of Educational Change in America* (New York: Praeger Publishers, 1971). Both of these books are reviewed in Vincent P. Franklin, "Historical Revisionism and Black Education," *School Review* 81 (May 1973), 477-86.

5. Ethnic Studies and Equality

Richard Kolm

The idea of equal general education is not exactly new. And the subject of ethnic studies was a popular political issue in Europe and South Asia at the beginning of this century. In the United States, the principles of public support and state responsibility in education were, in the main, already recognized and implemented by most of the states around the middle of the nineteenth century. The main theme of American educational policies after the Revolution centered around the ideas of freedom, equality, and democracy. The principles of government resting upon the consent of the governed called for an enlightened and responsible citizenry. The incorporation of the waves of immigrants arriving from the Old World, with their various cultural and social backgrounds, called for a common language to facilitate communication and to maintain social order; it called also for equalizing principles, rewarding individual abilities and de-emphasizing Old World social class concepts or national origins.

Thus, though the Constitution does not mention education, the idea of equal educational opportunity took hold and was implemented through a general public educational system. Public support, state control, and freedom from sectarianism were the three main objectives of the new American educational system, formulated in the nineteenth century. However, private schools, sponsored mainly by denominational and ethnic groups, were not forbidden and continued to exist and to develop.

Through emphasis on common language and group citizenship, the public schools became primary agents for fostering unity in American society. But with time, and particularly during the periods of intensive Americanization before World War II, the positive emphasis on unity through language and laws became a vehicle of the assimilationist and melting pot theories, emphasizing repression of cultural differences. Ideas of unity of language and law ultimately led to policies of cultural nationalism[1] thoroughly implemented by the educational system through curricula, textbooks, and teacher training.

The principle of equal educational opportunity broke down, however, over the issue of education for blacks. The historical sequence is well known—the often reluctant provision of education for blacks after the Civil War, the establishment of the segregationist principle of "separate but equal," the Supreme Court's decision in 1954, which declared that segregation in schools was "inherently a denial of equality of educational opportunity and thus prohibited by the fourteenth amendment to the U.S. Constitution." And we all are witnesses to the final act of desegregation in the American public school system. The drama only began with the black revolution in the sixties; it continues as one of the major problems of the nation.

At the same time other racial groups, mainly the Chicanos, raised the problem of handicaps in learning experienced by their children who, speaking Spanish at home, have great difficulties in following the demands of the public school curriculum. In response to these always existing but newly surfaced social needs caused by poverty, discrimination, or cultural disadvantages, a number of new programs and approaches were developed to ameliorate the situation. Two of these—black studies programs and the bilingual program—are most relevant here.

Black studies. The phenomenal growth of black studies over the past few years can only be interpreted as a need strongly felt by blacks and recognized by society, even if not always spontaneously. In a recent publication on *Ethnic Studies in Higher Education* published by the American Association of State Colleges and Universities, 477 colleges are listed as offering black studies; 141 of these, or over one-third, are programs in black studies (major or minor) and 69 of them, or about one-seventh, are degree programs. Some estimates go to as high as 400 for institutions of higher learning offering courses only, and about 200 offer independent programs in black studies.

The emphasis in these programs is on black history, literature, and interdisciplinary courses, in that order. A variety of purposes is being served by the programs and by individual writers in stressing the advantages of black studies both for the black population and for the whole society. Such studies provide an opportunity for blacks to understand their culture and heritage; to explore the social, political, and economic approaches for helping black people; to correct negative self-concepts held by blacks; to develop black identity; to enhance the black self-concept; to promote the cultural aspirations and stimulate the creativity of blacks. As for advantages to society, black studies increase understanding among the races and, consequently, combat discrimination and prejudice and reduce racial tensions.

Despite continuous controversy over the quality of these offerings, the qualifications of instructors, the racial composition of classes, and the problems of staffing and administrative control, it is generally accepted that black studies will remain a permanent ingredient of the higher education curriculum. Nearly all educators believe "that the ultimate and ideal way to handle materials on blacks and other ethnic groups is to weave them into the regular curricula as an integral part of everything that is taught from kindergarten to grade twelve." The emergence of black studies also constitutes the most common student-initiated change in the academic curriculum. The impact is said to be greatest on the community college where it "constitutes the most extensive modification of curriculum since addition of vocational-technical courses decades ago."

Many black studies programs, particularly those organized independently, appear to have been funded from outside sources, mainly foundations, whereas single courses are being absorbed locally, particularly by state colleges and universities.

Though only incomplete information is available on other racial minorities, it is evident that they have been following the example of black studies both with regard to expanding existing programs and to establishing new ones. The National Council for Chicano Studies estimates that about 150 interdisciplinary Chicano programs are

offered in institutions of higher education. In addition, twelve Chicano colleges have been formed and are affiliated with accredited
institutions. Program offerings are increasing in the Midwest and in
the Northwest. Similar increases in course offerings to study the
culture of the American Indian and other racial minorities can be
assumed.

Inclusion of ethnic content is also being demanded at the elementary and secondary school level. Some states already have legislation or policy statements requiring ethnic studies in the elementary
and secondary schools. Other states are developing guidelines or
adopting resolutions on the subject. As a result, there is a great need
for increased emphasis on training teachers for ethnic studies and
developing multiethnic materials.[2]

Bilingual education. The bilingual education program was established under Title VII of the Elementary and Secondary Education
Act of 1965 (Public Law 89-N) as amended in 1967 (Public Law
90-247) to meet the special educational needs of children who have
limited English-speaking ability. Officially, *bilingual education* means
"the use of two languages, one of which is English, as mediums of
instruction."[3] In the words of the report on the status and operation
of the ESEA, Title VII, for the fiscal year 1969:

The program is designed to serve children from low income families who come
from environments where the dominant language is other than English. . . . Use
of the mother tongue as well as English as the mediums of instruction, and the
study of the history and culture associated with the child's first language are
considered integral parts of bilingual education. . . .

Use of the dominant language thus prevents the academic retardation that
results if the children are not given any instruction in these subjects until they
learn English or if instruction is provided only through an English curriculum. In
addition, mastering the language arts of their own languages, especially reading
and writing, actually facilitates learning these skills in English after the children
have achieved sufficient command of oral English.

Moreover, language is intimately associated with one's concept of self and
with feelings of group identity. By accepting and recognizing the home language
and by using it for the children's learning experiences, bilingual programs provide a learning environment in which a more favorable self concept may be
developed and in which successful experiences rather than rejection and failure
are the rule. . . .

The law specifies that local educational agencies include in approved projects
children who are from environments where English is the dominant language if
such participation would enhance the effectiveness of the project. Accordingly,

projects have been encouraged to include English speaking children to the greatest extent possible.

Special policies have been developed for projects involving American Indian languages. . . .

The program stresses educational accountability, evaluation, and dissemination in the community. Activities are aimed at "comprehensiveness in scope, and they deal not only with the academic development of children in pre-school through grade twelve, but also with the education of their parents, the children's personal and social growth, relevant teaching styles and strategies, the working out of bilingual curriculum materials and guides and better home school relationships."[4]

The program also provides for training of teachers and teacher-aides (preservice and in-service), for the development of instructional materials, and for vertical expansion of projects, as well as for inclusion of new geographic areas and languages. The long-range goals of the bilingual program are best formulated, however, in the *Manual for Project Applicants and Grantees:*

—Students from the non-English-speaking environment will have an adult literate command of both languages.

—Students from the English-speaking environment will have an adult literate command of both languages.

—Students from the non-English-speaking environment will progress through the school program at the rate commensurate with that of English-speaking students of comparable ability.

—Students from the non-English-speaking environment will feel pride in their language and heritage.

—As great a percentage of those from the non-English-speaking environment as from the English-speaking environment will graduate from high school.

—As great a percentage of students from the non-English-speaking environment as from the English-speaking environment will enter college.

—Students from the non-English-speaking environment who choose not to pursue higher education will have the skills to secure employment in an English-speaking culture.

—All participants will value a multi-cultural society.

—A bilingual staff of teachers and administrators, many from the minority culture, will have developed the attitudes and skills to maintain an effective bilingual program.

—Parents from the non-English-speaking environment will participate as fully in school-related activities as those from the English-speaking environment.[5]

Grants for bilingual education are awarded on a competitive basis through a two-stage submission and approval process consisting of submission and review of preliminary proposals and later of comprehensive plans for the implementation of the proposed program by the selected local educational agencies.

In fiscal year 1969, 7.5 million dollars were appropriated for the Bilingual Education Program, seventy-six formal proposals in twenty-two states were finally approved and funded; of these, sixty-eight are designed to serve Spanish-speaking children; five, the American-Indians; two each, Portuguese and Chinese; one each, French and Japanese. A total of 26,521 children are participating in the program, representing approximately 8 percent of the total number of children with limited English-speaking ability in the target areas. Of these children, 95 percent are enrolled in public schools; 5 percent are enrolled in nonpublic schools.

The report concluded that approximately five million school age children have limited English-speaking ability and are in dire need of bilingual education. Only 27,000 were served in fiscal year 1969 through the bilingual education projects funded under the Elementary and Secondary Education Act, Title VII, at a cost of 7.5 million dollars. By projecting the funding to the total number of children, the total cost would be at least $400 million, apart from the cost of training of teachers. If there were twenty-five students per teacher and $1,000 were spent to train each teacher, program costs would increase by $200 million. It would require at least $600 million to provide bilingual education programs for all of the children in the nation who need them.[6]

It is not known how the estimated number of five million children was arrived at. However, according to the Census Bureau's *Current Population Report* for November 1969, which included characteristics of the population by ethnic origin, nearly thirty-six million Americans reported their mother tongue (that is, the language reported spoken at home during childhood) as non-English, though only twelve million of these reported a non-English language as their "current" language (language reported as the one usually spoken in the home at the time of the survey).[7] It could well be that, out of the twelve million, five million or more were children of school age. Even if we assume that many of these five million children would be Spanish- or French-speaking or Indians, it still would leave a sizable number—perhaps 2.5 million children, or more—with limited English-speaking ability.

Who are these children? They come mainly from the homes of the foreign born, frequently recent immigrants, mainly Europeans, Latin Americans with other than Spanish backgrounds, and Asians. They may also come from closely knit ethnic communities—Chinese, Japanese or other Asian communities—but they also come from groups of European origin—Italians, Greeks, Poles, Ukrainians, and others. A recent survey conducted in a Chicago school with an enrollment of 1,018 children discovered that the first language of 263 children was Greek.

Most of these children, however, will not get the needed assistance either because the concentration in one school area is too low or because their families have incomes slightly higher than the prescribed limit. In any case, the Bilingual Act excludes all those children from ethnic groups who come from homes where the "current language" may be English—at least as officially reported—but who may also use their mother tongue at home and would greatly need bilingual instruction to prevent their academic retardation. Such children would also need some study of their heritage to provide them with a learning environment "in which a more favorable self concept may be developed and in which successful experiences rather than rejection and failure are the rule."[8]

Furthermore, the Bilingual Act does not include all those coming from families who, though English is exclusively spoken, still identify themselves with their ethnic origins and who would be interested in the history and culture of their ancestors and benefit from it, both in their personal development and, most likely, also in their learning efficiency.

It is because of these limitations that the act is considered as not fulfilling its implicit promise of a basic change in "language policy" from an earlier intolerant tradition of assimilation to a new trend of favoring ethnic language maintenance and cultural pluralism. In addition, it is asserted that an analysis of the programs funded under the act shows that most of them are aimed directly at assimilation through ethnic-language shift rather than at the proclaimed program goals. Some describe it as being nothing more than a "disguised" assimilation program. Despite these shortcomings regarding eligibility provisions and implementation, the act provides for programs which, if made universally applicable and properly implemented, could benefit ethnic American, if not all American, children.

According to the Bureau of Census survey, 75 million Americans identified themselves in 1969 with one of the seven specific origins constituting the largest ethnic groups in the United States. Counting all those under "others" (53.3 percent of the population) who identified themselves with the remaining seventy-odd ethnic origins existing in the United States, we may well come up with a much larger figure, even if we subtract all those who have no interest whatsoever in any bilingual program, either because of lack of identification or, perhaps, unwillingness to identify with any ethnic origin.

But ethnic origin does not necessarily mean ethnic identification. In fact, we know very little about the ethnics in our society and their identification with their backgrounds. Origin is probably one of the most decisive factors, though even origin can be a controversial matter subject to ideological and situational factors as, for instance, was the case with pre-World War I immigrants from the Austrian, Russian and German states. Participation in ethnic life, involvement in group functions, and, finally, conscious commitment, are probably the best indexes of the dimensions of ethnic identification, but these will hardly be assessed by a census survey.

Most important, however, from the point of view of educational needs and equal opportunities is the attitude of society toward ethnic backgrounds and cultural differences in general. Two hundred years of absorption ideologies, whether bearing the assimilation brand or the melting pot designation, have conditioned the relational climate in American society and have left deep wounds, of which the recent racial unrest is only the most extreme and the most visible expression. In the final analysis it can be asserted that it was this absorptionist ideology which divided Americans into those recognized as meltable and those who were not. In other words it was a division into those who could hope to "make it" and become indistinguishable in American society, sharing in its prosperity, and those condemned to a life without hope. It was this division that provided the setting for the black revolution as the only means to break out of the vicious encirclement of dehumanization and hopelessness.

Conditions among the "meltables," however, were not ideal either. Strict ranking by their perceived "social distance" from the dominating groups was accompanied often by overt and covert, explicit and

implicit prejudice and discrimination. Through crude and subtle ethnic slurs and jokes, through slights in personal relations, in public life
and especially by means of the mass media, an atmosphere was created which pressured ethnics toward conformity to a generalized
abstract personality model. Such an atmosphere often compelled,
and still compels, children of ethnic families to reject their parents,
refuse to speak the language they learned in childhood at home, and
to disassociate themselves from the ethnic communities in which
they grew up.

The most critical moment for the ethnic child occurs when he first
enters school. He suddenly realizes that his cultural background has
little value in the outside world. At best, he hears little if anything
about it. Soon he learns that his background may be a handicap to
him, to his personal development, and to his future. This may be
conveyed to him not so much by the teacher, but by his peers. In
daily interaction the various reactions of the adult world are trans-
mitted. Here is what a girl from Maine writes about her childhood
school experiences.

I grew up in a New England city where French, Irish and Old English families
held a tight, economic and social control over the community. The few Polish
and Lithuanian families living there had to be content with menial, poor-paying
jobs and endure the condescension of their neighbors. Some of the children were
as biased as their parents; they mocked and scoffed at our Slavic ancestry openly
in their loud clear voices. Our teachers were impatient with our long names and
constantly misspelled and mispronounced them.

I grew up restrained and mouselike, dreading to make any movement or noise
that would call attention to myself. Only the warmth of our family life made the
harsh attitude of the community and the cold, unfriendly winters during those
depressing years bearable. My fifth grade history teacher was an elderly woman. . . . One day this cool, aloof teacher mentioned casually (we had been studying the American Revolutionary War for some weeks) that two Polish patriots
had come to America to help in the struggle for freedom. (She) said that she
thought it was quite wonderful that they had come such a long distance to help
and that it was a very generous gesture. . . .

I sat stunned. Unbelievingly, I absorbed the information and committed it to
memory. It was the first time I had heard something favorable about Poles
spoken in English. . . . I felt proud and happy and a little sad because I knew
that this wonderful moment would soon be over.[9]

In a metropolitan university where I taught for several years and
where most of the students were of ethnic origin, I found a high

correlation between the ethnicity of the students and their unwillingness to speak up in class. Those with the strongest ethnicity were also
the last ones to admit their background, even if the subject of ethnicity was discussed. In private conversations and conferences most of
them had similar stories to that of the girl mentioned above regarding
their experiences in elementary and high school. Similar experiences
are recounted by most ethnic adults. The message that the school
conveyed was very clear. To be a full-fledged American, one should
forget one's background, language, and grandparents. Fishman, writing on child indoctrination for minority-group membership thus describes the ethnic child in the school:

The assumptions posit a compelling American core culture, toward which the
minority-group child has ambivalent feelings. He is attracted to it, surrenders
willingly to it, desires to participate fully in it. The imperfect congruence between his aspirations and the possibility of his being absorbed generates ambiva-
lence whenever he is rejected. Nevertheless, the minority-group child is ever ready
to swallow his pride and try once more.[10]

Numerous studies and articles have repeatedly referred to this aspect of American education. Though most of these, particularly during the last decade, focused on the blacks, Mexicans, and other racial
minorities, quite a few of them refer to white ethnic groups. They
deal with phenomena such as the persistence of ethnic patterns;[11] the
significance of ethnicity to self-concept, to behavior, and in social
and personal disorganization;[12] language maintenance and group
maintenance related to social maladjustment;[13] ethnicity and school
adjustment and achievements.[14]

Inequality in American education with regard to ethnic children
still exists. The focus on racial minority groups and Mexican-Ameri-
cans is fully justified, and there is a similar need for extending such
programs to white ethnic groups. And, though no direct comparison
can be made to the experiences of the blacks in particular, there is a
psychological similarity in the experiences of white ethnic groups that
calls for attention and for remedial action through the schools.

The black studies and the bilingual programs, though they have
limitations, also have direct application to the needs of the white
ethnic groups. Perhaps a combination of both programs should be
made available, not only to those in need of it for self-development
and motivation for learning, but to all American children. Such inter-

cultural experience in school would promote the development of personal identity, increase interpersonal effectiveness, and develop communicative abilities in children.

The merits of a culturally pluralistic framework for American society with regard to both its form and content can be discussed, but the reality of American society and culture as being ethnically and racially diversified cannot be denied.

This reality has recently been recognized by Congress in the passage of the Ethnic Heritage Program in 1972. Though the program was not funded, as the administration did not ask for any of the authorized funds, the bill remains to document a decision by the representatives of the nation and as a source for reference. Its two fundamental precepts must be recognized as the cornerstones for any work in the field of ethnic studies:

1. American society is pluralistic, both historically and contemporaneously.
2. Cultural pluralism, if properly understood and implemented, is essentially positive, constructive, and conducive to higher human development and achievements.

The bill provides four definite criteria for activities, including development and dissemination of curriculum materials, providing training for teachers, and cooperation with community.

Meanwhile, however, the problem of ethnic studies is not dormant. States and communities have adopted measures, introduced either by the state legislatures, by local boards of education, or by mandates issued by state superintendents. Some state and local school systems have already made considerable progress in curricular and methodological development of ethnic studies. Much still remains to be done, including research not only on the educational aspects of ethnicity but also on American ethnicity itself. It is most important, however, that ethnicity be recognized and accepted as reality by American society and that ethnic studies be accepted and recognized, not just as an expressed need of any particular ethnic group but as a need of all Americans to know and understand themselves and each other and to achieve unity and social peace.

Notes

1. Joshua A. Fishman, *Language Loyalty in the United States* (The Hague: Mouton & Co., 1966), 29-31.

2. Winnie Bengelsdorf, *Ethnic Studies in Higher Education* (Washington, D. C.: American Association of State Colleges and Universities, 1972), 18, 33-93, 20, 37, 8, 41, 8.

3. U.S. Department of Health, Education, and Welfare, Office of Education (HEW-395), *Grants for Bilingual Education Programs* (Washington, D.C.: U.S. Government Printing Office, 1969), 1 (pamphlet).

4. U.S. Department of Health, Education, and Welfare, Office of Education, *Focus on Bilingual Education*, A Report on the Status and Operation of the Elementary and Secondary Education Act, Title VII, Fiscal Year 1969 (Washington, D.C.: U.S. Government Printing Office, 1971), 1.

5. U.S. Department of Health, Education, and Welfare, Office of Education Publication No. 4491-6, *Programs under Bilingual Education Act* (Title VII, Elementary and Secondary Education Act), *Manual for Project Applicants and Grantees*, April 20, 1971 (Washington, D. C.: U.S. Government Printing Office, 1972), 29-30.

6. U.S. Department of Health, Education, and Welfare, Office of Education, *Focus on Bilingual Education*, 34.

7. U.S. Bureau of the Census, *Characteristics of the Population by Ethnic Origin, November, 1969*, Series P-20, No. 271, 1971, p. 10.

8. James F. Redmond, General Superintendent of Schools, Board of Education of the City of Chicago, *Budlong Bilingual Child-Parent Center*, A Preliminary Proposal for Elementary and Secondary Education Act Title VII or Any Other Funding Source (Chicago: Chicago Board of Education, January 28, 1973), 4, 5-6.

9. *Poland* (November 1971), 20.

10. Joshua A. Fishman, "Childhood Indoctrination for Minority-Group Membership," *Daedalus* 90 (Spring 1961), 330.

11. For example, see Nathan Glazer and Daniel P. Moynihan, *Beyond the Melting Pot* (Cambridge, Mass.: M.I.T. Press, 1963), Introduction to the second edition.

12. For example, see William J. Goode, "Illegitimacy, Anomie and Cultural Penetration," *American Sociological Review* 26 (December 1961), 920-25.

13. For example, see Joshua A. Fishman, "The Ethnic Group School and Mother Tongue Maintenance in the United States," *Sociology of Education* 37 (Summer 1964), 306-17.

14. For example, see James G. Anderson and Dwight Safar, "The Influence of Differential Community Perceptions on the Provision of Equal Educational Opportunities," *Sociology of Education* 40 (Summer 1967), 219-30.

6. The Federal Politics of Bussing

Don T. Martin and *Robert Morgart*

In order to understand the complex issue of bussing and equal educational opportunity, it is first necessary to examine the political context in which it occurs. Central to the politics of bussing is the role of the federal government, and, more specifically, the influence of the Office of the President. As is well known, Richard Nixon has frequently voiced strong opposition to bussing.

Shortly after Nixon took office in 1969, there were overt signs of a policy that would alter the desegregation efforts of Lyndon Johnson's administration.[1] Nixon's early failure to slow desegregation policies in the South apparently frightened southern politicians.[2] Governor George Wallace of Alabama continued to provide ideological leadership, especially on the issue of bussing, but many politicians preferred to have a spokesman in Washington, a place of greater political significance than Montgomery.

By 1970, when the federal courts increased their efforts to reduce glaring racial imbalances in the nation's schools, Nixon said:

An expanded version of this essay was originally presented as a paper at the American Educational Studies Association meeting in Washington, D.C., November 2-3, 1972.

Considering the heavy demands for more school operative funds, I believe it is preferable, when we have to make the choice, to use limited financial resources for the improvement of education—for better teaching facilities, better methods, and advanced educational materials and for the upgrading of the disadvantaged area in the community rather than buying tires and gasoline to transport young children miles away from their neighborhood schools.[3]

After the United States Supreme Court unanimously upheld the constitutionality of bussing for desegregation purposes in 1971, an officer of the Department of Justice appointed by Nixon proposed an antibussing amendment as a means of intervening against the implementation of court-ordered bussing.[4]

The Florida presidential primary and referendum in March 1972 surely worried Nixon and his aides as George Wallace became more popular with his anti-"forced" bussing sentiments,[5] and more appealing to a large bloc of potential conservative Nixon supporters.[6] Even former civil rights advocate Senator Henry Jackson, who several months earlier had proposed an antibussing amendment in the Senate, was vying for the Wallace vote.

Nixon moved immediately to take political advantage of a growing national antibussing sentiment. In a nationwide radio and television address two days after the Florida primary he proposed a moratorium on bussing, and the urgency of the matter led him to abandon contemplation of a constitutional amendment:

There are many who believe that a constitutional amendment is the only way to deal with this problem. The constitutional amendment proposal deserves a thorough consideration by the Congress on its merits. But as an answer to the immediate problem we face of stopping more busing now, *the constitutional amendment approach has a fatal flaw. It takes too long.*

Instead of an amendment Nixon proposed "legislation that would call an immediate halt to all new busing orders by Federal Courts, a moratorium on new busing."

While opposing the unpopular issue of bussing, Nixon verbalized support for equal educational opportunity by stating that "at the same time that we stop more busing, we move forward to guarantee that the children currently attending the poorest schools in our cities and in rural districts be provided with education equal to that of the good schools in their communities." He justified both legislative proposals by declaring that: "The issue of busing divides many Americans . . . but . . . the commitment to equal opportunity in education unites all Americans. . . . The proposals I am submitting to Congress will allow us to turn away from what divides us and to turn toward what unites us."[7]

Nixon recognized that Florida voters, while giving Wallace a landslide victory, cast 74 percent of their votes in a referendum against "forced bussing" and yet 79 percent of the vote favored equal educational opportunity. It seems more than a coincidence that Nixon's requests for a bussing moratorium and equal educational opportunity were consistent with the results of the Florida referendum. The two legislative proposals were, from our viewpoint, consistent with most other Nixon legislative proposals affecting health, education, and welfare—contradictory and based mainly on political expediency.

The moratorium bill, which would have stopped new bussing orders by federal courts until July 1, 1973, would have violated the due process clause of the Fourteenth Amendment, in the opinion of a number of legal scholars, including former Associate Supreme Court Justice Arthur Goldberg. In effect, it would have given Congress the authority to regulate the courts. Such a violation of the highest law of the land seemed contradictory, indeed, since it came from such a strong supporter of law and order.

The proposed Equal Educational Opportunity Act, providing $2.5 billion for poor rural and urban schools, was inconsistent with Nixon's prior opposition to spending in this area.[8] Actually, no new money was ever proposed in this act. The funds would have come from federal programs already existing (Title I of the 1965 Elementary and Secondary Education Act) or those near enactment. The President supported such aid as long as it did not dip into the federal treasury. Nixon deplored most spending measures in the human resource category as inflationary, but simultaneously pushed for the largest defense budget ($76 billion) since World War II.

The long battle over the passage of the bussing moratorium bill ended in a liberal Senate filibuster. Senate minority leader, Hugh Scott, a driving force behind Nixon's legislation in Congress, not only voted against cloture, but he apparently was one of the most powerful forces behind the filibuster. Surely if Nixon had wanted the bill to pass he could have pressured Scott and most moderate northern Republican senators to vote for cloture. Only those up for re-election, such as Senators Baker and Griffin, did so. Even southern senators who voted for cloture could not have been satisfied with the bill since they were apparently more interested in reopening previous desegregation cases than in stopping new court orders that would primarily affect the North. What appeared to be the defeat of a Nixon-sponsored bill was in fact a political victory for him.

Southern senators could now blame the defeat of the bill on northern liberals, and, at the same time, look forward to beginning the fight anew in the next Congress—a Congress they hoped would be more conservative in the event of a Nixon landslide. A conservative Congress might pass a much stronger antibussing bill. Not only could a permanent bussing ban be enacted, but the bill could even include provisions for reopening former desegregation cases. Such a bill would have pleased southerners who were living with past court-ordered bussing mandates. Had this happened, it might have restored segregated schools in the South and retained de facto segregation in the North. Thus, Nixon's second term would, in a very real sense, have been comparable to the post-Civil War anti-Reconstruction policies of Andrew Johnson and Rutherford B. Hayes. The South would have had cause to be even more grateful to Nixon-Agnew-style Republican politics for many years to come, and Nixon and his benefactors would have won the South over to the Republican party, supplanting the political leadership of the ailing George Wallace.

Although Nixon spoke of a commitment to guarantee rural and urban poor school children an education equal to that of the privileged, the legislative record of his administration does not suggest that the commitment was very strong. The Equal Educational Opportunity Act, proposed in 1972, would perhaps be more properly titled the Unequal Educational Opportunity Act of 1972. But being at least rhetorically on the side of equal educational opportunity was still popular among most voters and politicians.

What did equal educational opportunity really mean for many Americans and for Nixon? It certainly did not mean equal inputs (funds, facilities, teachers' salaries, and so forth) to the schools, for there were vast educational inequalities on the state and local levels, and even within individual schools. A child from Harlan, Kentucky, simply does not have the same educational opportunity that a Scarsdale, New York, child has; nor does an East Los Angeles child have educational opportunity equal to that of a child from Beverly Hills.

Recent research has called attention to the traditional fallacy of considering equal educational opportunity almost exclusively from an input level. Concern has been redirected to output (the benefits derived from an educational experience in the schools). The Coleman Report[9] claimed that what occurs in schools in terms of educational achievement does not matter nearly as much as what occurs in the home and in the child's total environment. Sociologist David Armor, when at Harvard, generally developed the same thesis.[10] While supporting the idea of "voluntary bussing," Armor warned, however, that not much could be expected in the way of educational change from bussing.

One could conclude from these and some other studies that compensatory programs and bussing were of little if any educational value as they related to providing equal economic opportunity, which is what equal educational opportunity is supposed to result in eventually. Nixon used these studies in several of his speeches to support an austere budget for compensatory educational programs. Apparently Nixon and his advisers chose to ignore Christopher Jencks's final conclusions in *Inequality*: "our research does not justify cutting school reform expenditures, abandoning desegregation or giving up efforts at school reform."[11]

In an antibussing speaking tour throughout the country, Irene McCabe of Pontiac, Michigan, spokeswoman for the National Action Group (NAG), frequently referred specifically to Armor's Boston METCO study in order to further the NAG position that bussing would not result in higher levels of educational achievement, and that, furthermore, it would produce more racial friction.[12] Armor compared a group of thirty-two bussed students with a control group of sixteen who were not bussed. McCabe deliberately emphasized the short-term effects of bussing, but she ignored that part of Armor's study dealing with long-term educational effects. Armor had concluded that "bused students were very much more likely to start college than the control group . . . The METCO program seems to have had a dramatic effect upon the impetus for college, and many more of the bused students actually started some form of higher education." Armor found, however, that, by the end of their sophomore year, 59 percent of the bussed students were still in school, but so also were 56 percent of the nonbussed students. Armor further noted that:

In spite of this higher drop out rate, the bused students were still enrolled in what are generally considered higher-quality institutions. That is, 56 percent of the bused students were in regular four-year colleges, compared to 38 percent for the control (non-bused) group. An even greater difference was found for those enrolled in full universities (which include a graduate school).

Armor also pointed out that similar findings were obtained in an unpublished special college follow-up study of the ABC (A Better Chance) program. Referring to this study done in 1972 by George Perry and to his own work, Armor concluded that there seemed to be

some strong evidence that middle-class suburban or prep schools have an important "channeling" effect not found in black schools. The effect is probably due to better counseling and better contacts with college recruiting officers. Whatever the reason, black students attending such schools may have doors opened for them that are closed to students attending predominantly black schools. Given the lack of positive effects in other areas, these findings may have great significance for future busing programs, and future research is urgently needed.[13]

Henry Dyer underscored the need for research on bussing when he claimed that the "Hartford experiment is the only one that can be considered a true experiment . . . on the actual effects . . . of busing."[14] We, too, believe that the findings Armor refers to have great significance for future bussing programs and that further research is urgently needed.

The Coleman, Armor, and Jencks studies cited earlier have sparked controversies that are still raging among scholars deeply committed to the investigation of what actually constitutes equal educational opportunity. Both Coleman and Jencks have been concerned about the misuse of their findings. In an unpublished letter sent to *The New York Times* on April 13, 1972, Coleman expressed chagrin that the courts "inappropriately" used his report "to support the premise that equal protection for black children is not provided unless racial balance is achieved in schools." More importantly, Coleman said, "The Report found, as I have testified in various court cases, and as has been confirmed by numerous further analyses of those same data, that the academic achievement of children from lower socio-economic backgrounds (black or white) was benefited by being in schools with children from higher socio-economic backgrounds (black or white)."

However, Coleman acknowledged that the achievement increment was "not nearly sufficient to overcome the educational disadvantage of children from lower socio-economic backgrounds. This effect, however, was greater than those of other school resources of the kind ordinarily added by compensatory programs. The effects of these resources on achievement can hardly be found at all."[15] During an interview in preparation for an hour-long television documentary (in which he was subsequently to participate), Coleman was asked: "What constitutes equal educational opportunity?" He replied:

The classic definition explained educational equality in terms of inputs to schools—the quality of textbooks, size of classrooms, age of the physical plant, teacher training. Only recently has there been a shift to looking at the consequences of the school, looking at what schools really do, and how well children perform in their educational environment. When one looks at equality in terms of school outputs, a whole set of new factors must be examined . . . Quality education for children either of advantaged or disadvantaged backgrounds really depends upon experience with persons unlike themselves.[16]

When asked, "What does class segregation do to American society?" Coleman said:

Class integration . . . represents a fundamental break with the past because it asserts the importance of social choice over individual choice . . . (The) *research results indicate that a child's performance, especially a working-class child's performance, is greatly benefited by his going to school with children who come from educationally stronger backgrounds . . . When a working-class child is in this kind of school (upper-middle), he performs better than he would if in a homogeneous setting.* [17]

We agree with Coleman on this particular idea, and, therefore, believe that working-class children can benefit from association with other children from the middle- or upper-middle classes, and vice versa. But the society in which we live does not maximize such mixing, particularly in schools. Class-segregated schools dominate American education; they tend to mirror the class segregation of American society.

Radical change of our class-structured society could only occur with a major political revolution. This is not likely to occur; nor do we advocate such drastic change. But considerable change, we believe, can occur by other means such as a radical alteration of the present tax structure. This, we believe, would go to the heart of many of our present social inequalities. Schools need to be financed by some kind of federal or state tax levy which would be allocated to school districts according to the financial need of pupils therein.

We would like to suggest that, if we are interested in moving away from inequality in our schools to a meaningful degree of equality, we shall have to provide for significant class integration among our public schools. The only immediate means by which this could be accomplished is through cross-class bussing. Present bussing, we believe, has been destined to failure because it has too frequently pitted working-class whites against working-class blacks. Nixon and his political followers have profited from such class divisiveness.

The controversy over bussing became a national hysteria in 1972 and drove many political candidates to the right. But bussing was a false issue, and it still is. Of the twenty million students being bussed in the nation, fewer than 3 percent are bussed for purposes of racial integration, and of that percentage very few are bussed across class lines.

As late as September 1973 the President, in his second "State of the Union" message opposed bussing as "an unsatisfactory remedy for the inequities and inequalities of educational opportunity that exist in our country, tragic as those discrepancies are. We have been working to end those discrepancies and we will continue to do so."[18]

Whether or not Nixon has renewed his antibussing stance as a means to divert public attention from the severe problems of his administration is not as serious, we believe, as the implications of such a policy statement. Commitment to a rigid neighborhood concept and to antibussing has been and will continue to be a major setback to those efforts to provide for more equal educational opportunity. In order for our nation to attain greater educational equality, we must first declass our schools. Without this, attempts to equalize opportunity will be severely hampered.

Notes

1. Daniel P. Moynihan suggested to President Nixon as early as January 1969 that he proceed with a policy of "benign neglect" of racial minorities. This thesis stemmed originally from a series of lectures given by Moynihan in 1967 and subsequently published under the title *Maximum Feasible Misunderstanding: Community Action in the War on Poverty* (New York: Free Press, 1969). The book signaled Moynihan's departure from corporate-liberal social policy strategies and asked that we attribute the "failure" of the war on poverty programs to the victims of economic and racial injustice and not to the programs.

2. It now seems likely that Nixon did in fact assure Senator Strom Thurmond that, in return for southern conservative support in 1968, he would change the direction of the federal government's efforts for integration.

3. Quoted in *Phi Delta Kappan* 53 (No. 8, April 1972), 475. Nixon, of course, failed to mention the expensive cost of previous bussing for racial segregation in the South.

4. The officer was William H. Rehnquist, then an Assistant Attorney General and later an Associate Justice of the United States Supreme Court.

5. Wallace's speeches included such statements as, "We're going to shake their eyeteeth out . . . We're going to send them a message, those national Democrats." After his landslide victory, when asked what he would do with his votes, Wallace replied: "Well, I'd get me a room, sit in a chair, light up a cigar, get on the phone and call those boys up and tell them to come on up and see King George" (*New York Times*, March 17, 1972).

6. This occurred despite Florida Governor Ruben Askew's heroic effort to stem the antibussing tide.

7. *New York Times*, March 16, 1972, p. 22 [italics ours].

8. Two examples were (1) the first budget, fiscal 1970, provided only 39 percent of the authorized amount of funds for educationally deprived children, and (2) a consistent effort to cut the school lunch program.

9. Section 402 of the Civil Rights Act of 1964 instructed the United States Office of Education to conduct the second largest social science research project in history. A total of 570,000 school students were surveyed throughout the nation, and the results of the survey were revealed in a report, *Equality of Educational Opportunity*, commonly known as the Coleman Report. Since the release of this report in the summer of 1966, its controversial findings have stirred continual re-examination. Most notable perhaps are the papers derived from Harvard University's faculty seminar on the Coleman Report. See Frederick Mosteller and Daniel P. Moynihan (eds.), *On Equality of Educational Opportunity* (New York: Random House, 1972).

10. David Armor, "The Evidence on Busing," *The Public Interest* (No. 28, Summer 1972), 90-126.

11. *New York Times*, December 3, 1972.

12. After a debate on bussing at Carnegie Mellon University, in October 1972, we asked Ms. McCabe questions tangential to Armor's study; when pressed on the issue of equality, she declared emphatically that she did not believe in equal educational opportunity in any form.

13. Armor, *op. cit.*, 106.

14. See Mosteller and Moynihan, *op. cit.*, 410.

15. This letter was later published in "Coleman on the 'Coleman Report,'" *The Public Interest* (No. 28, Summer 1972), 127-28.

16. "An Interview with Dr. James S. Coleman," *Class . . . and the Classroom*, Urban America Unit, Group W (Westinghouse Broadcasting Company, 1972), p. 2, interviewed by Dick Hubert, producer-writer.

17. *Ibid.*, p. 3.

18. *New York Times*, September 10, 1973.

7. Opportunity, Equity, or Equality

Robert J. Havighurst

Christopher Jencks, in his book on inequality,[1] examines skeptically the belief that schooling operates as a major force to reduce the inequality with which children are born. He concludes that "the character of a school's output depends largely on a single input, namely the characteristics of the entering children. Everything else— the school budget, its policies, the characteristics of the teachers—is either secondary or completely irrelevant" (p. 256).

No wonder the reviews of this book appearing in educational journals have been overwhelmingly negative. Furthermore, the liberal press has reacted against it. In an editorial the *New York Times* says that the book would be useful if its authors were content to document the limitations of the school system as an instrument of social reform. "Regrettably, however, the report has a serious flaw as a policy guide for either educational or social reform. It proceeds on the false premise that there is an inherent contradiction between the belief in equality of opportunity for all and the acknowledgement of great individual differences in competence, aspirations, and effort."[2]

I have seen nine reviews or editorials commenting on the book.

This is an expanded version of an article that appeared in *School Review* 81 (August 1973), 618-33. Used with permission of the University of Chicago Press.

Seven are critical and negative. One is neutral. One is laudatory. This last is a column by right-wing commentator James J. Kilpatrick who says Jencks has told the truth about education, which is an "unpardonable sin" in the eyes of "the educationists." He says Jencks has "debunked" the assumption that, if schools are made substantially equal, poverty can be greatly reduced.[3] Thus Jencks gives support to the rightists who favor tax reduction through reducing school expenditures. If schooling does not pay off by increasing the incomes of the poor, why spend public money on it?

This is a book about equality, and it says that equality of educational opportunity does not and cannot go far enough toward producing equality of income. But it accepts the facts of inequality and asks only for a greater degree of economic equality among adults, gained through political methods. Jencks says, "Our commitment to equality is, then, neither all-embracing nor absolute. We do not believe that everyone can or should be made equal to everyone else in every respect. We assume that some differences in cognitive skill and vocational competence are inevitable. . . . But we also believe that the distribution of income can be made far more equal than it is, even if the distribution of cognitive skill and vocational competence remains as unequal as it is now" (p. 11).

Can education provide enough opportunity to enable the children of the poor and the disadvantaged to achieve a fair degree of equality of income when they become adults? This is the question to which the book answers, "No." It was written by the leader of a team of eight men and women, all under forty, nearly all under thirty, who worked in the Harvard University Center for Educational Policy Research. He says, "The present text was written by Christopher Jencks. It embodies his prejudices and obsessions, and these are not shared by all the co-authors" (p. v).

The book is aimed at a large audience but is heavy reading for a person not familiar with statistics. There are 130 pages of technical appendixes, which are valuable for a student of social statistics. Each of the eight substantive chapters has a voluminous set of notes, referring either to the appendixes or to articles and books which are mainly of a technical nature.

The substantive chapters report research on inequality: in the schools, in cognitive skills, in educational attainment (level of education), in occupational status, in money income, and in job satisfaction. The longest chapter, "Inequality in Cognitive Skills," is fifty-nine pages of text and twenty pages of 157 "notes." The shortest chapter is only three pages. It is on "Non-cognitive Traits," regarded by Jencks as very important in the determination of adult status and income. But, as he says, "This chapter is largely a confession of ignorance and a plea for rethinking our attitudes toward the schools."

There are no new research data reported in the book. Rather, it is an integration of available data collected from large samples and treated by sophisticated statistical techniques. The principal sources were the Coleman Equality of Opportunity Survey; Project Talent Survey of high school seniors of 1961 who were followed for five years after their graduation; the National Opinion Research Center Survey of military veterans in 1964; and the studies of occupational status and its correlates made by Duncan, Blau, and Riess, mainly with census data on white, nonfarm males born between 1897 and 1936. The decision to rely mainly on these large-scale studies had advantages. It also had some serious disadvantages, as I will explain later.

The book invites us to clarify our ideas about the output of the educational system, within which there is a complex set of interactions between family and socioeconomic background, inherited mental ability, cognitive skills, amount of formal education attained, personality or noncognitive traits, race, sex, and quality of schools. Does this system reduce the inequality which exists among children? Does it facilitate social mobility? In what ways might the educational system be changed to secure greater equality of income and social status within the generation it serves?

The Setting of the Book

More than in most universities, there is a vigorous controversy at Harvard between two points of view and two sociopolitical theories concerning the functions of the educational system in contemporary society. This controversy is between the "liberals" and the "young radicals."

Among the liberals are Daniel Patrick Moynihan, Daniel Bell, Seymour Martin Lipset, James Q. Wilson, Nathan Glazer, and Thomas Pettigrew. They favor liberal reforms within the developing postindustrial society. They believe that our society has become more democratic in important ways during the present century and that the educational system exercises a substantial influence through providing educational opportunity for children of the poor and the minority groups. They are pragmatic, arguing that social problems are complex and cannot be solved by educational reform alone. In a recent issue of *Public Interest,* several of them wrote on the problem in inequality.[4] They would attempt to reduce inequality of incomes by moderate political means, such as placing a floor under family incomes. They would expand opportunity for youth through educational means. However, they see a certain degree of inequality of competence, goals, and interests as inevitable and even beneficial, since a good society needs and rewards people with diverse skills and life styles.

The young radicals are discontented with the "conservatism" of the liberals. They want drastic changes in the society, and some of them believe that drastic educational changes can make a big difference in favor of greater equality and equity. There are a number of economists in this group, and some of them are loosely organized in the Union of Radical Political Economists. One of these is Herbert Gintis, a member of the Jencks team, and another is Samuel Bowles, with whom Gintis collaborated in a 1972 mimeographed working paper entitled "IQ in the United States Class Structure," distributed by the Harvard Center for Educational Policy Research. Another of this group who might be called "antiliberal" is David K. Cohen, whose 1970 article on "Immigrants and the Schools" contended that the American school system has systematically rejected the immigrant poor.[5]

From this distance it looks as if a considerable part of the Jencks team espouses the antiliberal position concerning the potential of the educational system for promoting equity or equality in American society. They do this from a position to the left of the liberals. But this may not be Jencks's own position. Although he appears to favor some form of socialistic redistribution of income, he is an ambivalent socialist. He has many doubts about the political feasibility of socialist controls over wages, salaries, and incomes, although he says he favors them. Jencks may be a man in the middle, between the two warring camps that are visible at Harvard and elsewhere. _____

There appear to be three ideological positions with respect to the effects of the school system in American society during the past century, each of which is supported by a considerable body of reliable and valid research.

Liberal position. School is an instrument conceived and used by a democratic society to maximize opportunity for the children of economically and socially disadvantaged groups to become more competent, more successful, and better-satisfied members of society. The system has difficulties in a complex and racist society, but liberals should believe in it and help to make it work better than it does today. This is the position of the Harvard liberals and of most members of the educational establishment. Liberals acknowledge the facts of inequality—of family position, inherited ability, and personality. Liberals believe that a good educational system can give substantial assistance to disadvantaged children and youth in moving toward the goal of a "better" economic position for themselves.

Radical left position. School, in spite of the good words spoken about it, is really an instrument used by the people in power to serve their purposes. The system favors their children and favors the political structure in which they have been successful. It accepts a limited number of "poor but able" youth and permits them to climb the socioeconomic ladder part way, thus perpetuating the Horatio Alger myth. But essentially it represents an effort by the upper-middle class to maintain its power and to pass this power on to their children. This is a simplification of what recent "revisionist" historians of education are saying, among them Colin Greer, Michael Katz, and several of the members of the Harvard Center for Educational Policy Research.

The two conflicting groups agree on one thing. The school system is effective in the functions it is supposed to serve—in the liberal interpretation to give opportunity to the children of the poor; in the radical interpretation to oppress them in favor of the children of the middle class.

"School is irrelevant" position. The position Jencks appears to hold is that school has very little influence, one way or another. The school system is a convenience for middle-class parents; it teaches their children the three R's, but their children get from school what the parents have prepared them to get. School does not give as much help to children of low-income parents, because these parents do not prepare their children for school through teaching them attitudes and habits that enable them to make effective use of the offerings.

Years of schooling are the important single determinant of level of occupational status. But educational attainment does not go far in determining a person's income. The variability of income for men within a given occupation is greater than the variability of incomes between occupational categories. Since Jencks is primarily interested in inequality of income, he must look to other causes than educational differences. He ascribes most of the differences between men's incomes to differences in personality, noncognitive skills, and luck.

Tone of the Book

The book has a cool tone, never strident or tendentious. In fact, it is so disarming that one finds oneself going along with the argument beyond the point one's critical judgment would ordinarily permit. The argument is always reasonable, sometimes with a slightly humorous twist. Jencks does not allow himself to complain about the cup being empty when he sees it is half full. So much of the educational situation today is like the cup which is half full, or half empty. In this condition it is not as good (full) as we might wish, but it is not as bad (empty) as it might be. A number of the more strident critics cry that the cup is empty, and this arouses the apologists for the educational establishment to shout that the cup is full.

Judged by the criterion of clarity of presentation, the book is an interesting mixture. There is frequently a simplifying summary following a turgid page of statistics. This saves the day for the less sophisticated reader, although it oversimplifies the data. In several places this kind of exposition plays down a really substantial difference that should be attributed to education. In the discussion of the possible effect of the school environment on students' desire to stay in school and get more education, Jencks argues that the quality of the school makes little difference. "Our best guess is that the cumulative impact of school quality alters the average student's educational attainment less than half a year" (p. 148). This is meant to say that the intraschool atmosphere and facilities have little or no effect on students' educational aspirations. But suppose we examine this statement. In a school of 1,000 which has a favorable environment for educational aspirations, let us assume that the average educational level reached by students (going to college, graduating from college) is raised by 0.5 year, or 500 student years. Assume a cross-sectional student body in terms of socioeconomic status. Some 400 students are sure to go on to college, no matter what the school is like. Some 200 students are sure to drop out of school before graduation, no matter what the school is like. Another 200 will go right to work or get married as soon as they graduate from high school. They are sure about this. Then there is a middle group of 200 students who are undecided and ambivalent about going to college. Suppose these are the only students influenced by the intraschool atmosphere, and they use the 500 student-years of college to get an average of 2.5 years of college. Then the statement about alteration of the "average" student's educational attainment by 0.5 year would actually mean that a sensitive fifth of the student body extended their education an average of 2.5 years beyond what they would have done in a school which made further education less attractive.

What the Book Says

The research team examined seven aspects of inequality in the experience of a person growing from youth to maturity, all of which are probably related to inequality of income. These areas of inequality are family socioeconomic status, educational opportunity, cognitive skills (IQ), educational attainment (level), noncognitive traits, job satisfaction, and occupational status (prestige).

A basic value assumption was that the present inequality of adult income (the top fifth of the population receives seven times as much income as the bottom fifth) was unjust in a democratic society. How, then, can the educational system operate to reduce the present degree of income inequality? The liberal hypothesis says that there is a close relationship among educational opportunity, cognitive skills, educational attainment, and adult income. If this is so, then expansion of educational opportunity for children of poor families and teaching them cognitive skills more effectively should reduce the present inequalities of adult income.

The book concludes that income inequality is stubborn and cannot be greatly reduced through changes in the educational system. However, critics of the book do not agree with this conclusion, as we shall see. But first it will be useful to look at some of the inequalities.

Inheritance of IQ. Inequalities of cognitive skills are related to some extent, at least, to inequalities in educational attainment and to inequalities in adult income. To what extent can inequalities in cognitive skills be reduced by better teaching? This question raises the issue of heritability of the IQ, which Jencks deals with directly. His results are generally acceptable to social scientists and to educators. The book devotes a fifty-page technical appendix to the task of "Estimating the Heritability of IQ Scores." Jensen estimated that 80 percent of the variance of IQ is inherited, and only 20 percent is due to environmental experience. Jencks concludes that only 45 percent of the variance of IQ scores is inherited, while 35 percent is due to environment. This leaves 20 percent to be explained by the interaction between heredity and environment. The child's environment is partially determined by his parents, and intellectually superior parents provide superior environments for their children. This section of the book will probably be reprinted and widely used. It answers Jensen and others who stress the importance of heredity and appears to draw on empirical studies more widely and more critically than Jensen does.

Comparison of school with family inputs. Family background or socioeconomic status tends to determine the level of cognitive skills of students to as great an extent as does inherited mental ability. The nature of the school, the amount of money spent on it, and/or the size of classes do not seem to have much influence on the cognitive-skill level of students of similar home background. But there is some evidence that the methods and resources of the school have a small influence on cognitive skills. Jencks encourages continued innovation in the belief that the schools can find ways of working more effectively, especially with disadvantaged youth. "If schools continue to use their resources as they do now, giving them more resources will not change children's test scores. If schools used their resources differently, however, additional resources might conceivably have larger payoffs" (p. 97).

Influence of schooling on occupational status. The largest single relationship found in this study is the one between amount of schooling (educational attainment) and adult occupational status. The correlation between a man's educational attainment and his occupational status is around 0.65. The correlation of adult scores on a test of cognitive skills with occupational status is about 0.50. The correlation between a father's occupational status and his son's status is about 0.48. These two factors (family background and cognitive skills) probably influence the amount of schooling a person will get.

But there are still enormous differences in occupational status among people with the same amount of education. Jencks claims that cognitive skills, family socioeconomic status, and amount of education, when put together, only account for half of the statistical variance in men's occupational status. This is one of the points where his critics disagree with him.

Influence of schooling and other factors on income. Jencks finds that income is considerably less dependent on family background, schooling, and cognitive test scores than is occupational status. Men born into the upper-middle class earn only 75 percent more than men born into the poorest fifth of families. But the richest fifth of all men in 1970 made at least 650 percent more than the poorest fifth. Thus variation in men's incomes is not explainable in terms of the factors studied in this research. Jencks says, "We estimate that there is nearly as much income variation among men who come from similar families, have similar credentials, and have similar test scores, as among men in general. This suggests either that competence does not depend primarily on family background, schooling, and test scores, or else that income does not depend on competence" (pp. 254-55).

What the Critics Say

From a liberal political position. Bayard Rustin, black executive director of the A. Philip Randolph Institute and cochairman of the Socialist Party-Democratic Socialist Federation, argues that Jencks does a disservice to liberal politics by questioning whether education can have any significant effect on the adult earning power of poor children. He says that Jencks's argument is utopian and defeatist. "He [Jencks] tells us that socialism is a necessary precondition to an equal society and then says that 'until we change the political and moral premises on which most Americans now operate, poverty and inequality will persist at pretty much their present level.' To accede to such an all or nothing view would be to acknowledge that the principles and goals of the civil rights movement have generated no more than so much wasted motion. And yet the evidence is clear that blacks have made quite substantial progress in education."[6]

The *Wall Street Journal*, an exponent of a liberal capitalist position, refers to Jencks in an editorial on the *Serrano* court decision which requires a reform in school financing to give inner-city schools stronger financial support. The *Journal* notes with approval that Jencks found that added school expenditures do not improve the school achievement of children (see the Coleman Report). But the *Journal* criticizes Jencks for wanting to reform the schools, anyway. "And that such findings [Coleman Report] do not quench the reformist instinct is demonstrated by Professor Jencks' own conclusion that since the schools do not end inequality, we need socialism. Now that he has learned something about the schools, the next thing he should study is socialism."[7]

From a sophisticated research position. A number of researchers who have worked with the same kinds of data and the same statistical techniques are less than happy with the methods and findings of this research. The most penetrating of these criticisms comes from Henry M. Levin, an economist-educationist at Stanford University. His review of the Jencks book in *Saturday Review/Education*[8] followed closely upon the appearance of a brief prepublication summary of the book in *Saturday Review/Education* for October 1972. Some of Levin's published research suggests that there is a strong relationship between success in school and occupational-economic success.[9] He says that many previous studies by economists find that both schooling and family background have substantial effects on adult earnings.[10] How is it possible, then, that Jencks's conclusions are in such sharp contrast to those of other researchers? "The answer seems to lie in differences in interpretation and in treatment of the data. For example, some differences that Jencks interprets as small ones would not seem trivial to other observers."[11] But the more serious discrepancies between Jencks and other competent researchers are due to differences in the statistical treatment of the data. "The book's principal finding on the inefficacy of schools is that test scores, family background, and related factors account for only 12-15 percent of differences in income. In contrast other studies have found that from one-third to one-half of the variance in income can be explained by these and similar influences. . . . The *Inequality* study omitted data that would have improved considerably the amount of variance in income inequality."[12] Jencks did not include data on age and place of residence in his analysis. These account for much of the variance of income. By ignoring them, Jencks increases the amount of "unexplained" variance of income.

In the application of sophisticated statistics to the kind of data analyzed by Jencks, the researcher must use his judgment to make many decisions that might differ from those made by another equally competent researcher. His own values and biases control his findings. Levin sums it up: "Though Jencks gives the impression that his results are derived strictly from his statistical model and social-science methodology, in fact, the application of that model and its methodology are based upon numerous judgments and opinions. . . . the actual findings and interpretations are at least as much a product of the value perspectives and opinions of the researcher as they are of the methodology and data. Unfortunately, the values and biases of the researcher are built into his procedures and interpretations at every stage."[13]

From a social-psychological position. The experts in social-psychological studies of educational performance in relation to social class and school factors are likely to be dissatisfied with some of Jencks's findings because of the limitations imposed by the nature of his data and his samples. Jencks used the best large-scale studies he could find and used data from questionnaires filled out by the subjects, not from interviews, observations, or other sources that might have given more depth to the data. This was a defensible procedure, since it gave him large numbers, with fairly reliable data. But it also omitted some important data. My own thirty years of experience studying the relations of social class or socioeconomic status to amount of schooling and to achievement on intelligence tests lead me to doubt the adequacy of some of his data to substantiate some of his interpretations. In his study of the relationship *between father's occupational status and son's educational level, occupational status and income,* Jencks uses the data from a major study reported by Blau and Duncan of white nonfarm males born between 1897 and 1936.[14] There were 45 million men in this age group in 1962, when the study was made, but 12 million had fathers who were farmers and farm laborers and were omitted from the study. No blacks were included. Thus the findings reported by Jencks apply only to white males who were not born on farms.

Jencks is aware of the problem. "The exclusion of farm-born whites and of all blacks restricts the range of variation in most variables and lowers the correlations somewhat. A comparison between correlations reported in Duncan, Featherman, and Duncan, *Socioeco-*

nomic Background, for white males, white nonfarm males, and black males and correlations reported in Blau and Duncan, *The American Occupational Structure,* for all nonfarm males suggests that the differences between nonfarm whites and the total population are quite small. The results for blacks are, however, quite different from those for whites" (p. 322).

Actually, the relationship between education and income for blacks is an example of the fact that this relationship varies a great deal among ethnic and geographical subgroups. In an article not reported by Jencks, Daniel P. Moynihan reports a study by Andrew Brimmer, one of the governors of the Federal Reserve Bank, on this question. In the one year from 1967 to 1968, the median income of Negro families headed by a person with *any* college experience rose from $8,686 to $10,704. For comparable whites, the median income rose only from $11,548 to $12,356. In 1968 Negro families headed by an adult with one to three years of college had a median income 111.1 percent higher than that of Negro families whose head had one to three years of high school. For whites in similar groups, the gap was only 29.6 percent. Thus the relation of education to income was greater in the black than in the white subgroups. This was partly due to the push of civil rights legislation toward opening better-paying jobs to blacks. It also indicates that interpretations of data for white males are not likely to apply to black males.

Another inadequacy in Jencks's data is his omission of women in his statistical studies. There are eleven references to women in the index. Nine of them are found in the chapter on income inequality. Tables 7-2, 7-4, and 7-5 actually give data on female earnings, but there is no analysis of them in relation to education (pp. 213, 222, and 225).

The individual versus the statistical. As one of many who have studied individuals intensively as they grow from childhood to adulthood, I am unsatisfied by a heavy reliance on data from statistical studies of large groups based on questionnaires which are bound to be superficial. I know that such studies are useful in dealing with very general questions. But they miss the real connections between family, schooling, personality, IQ, and peer group on the one hand, and adult occupational and economic attainment on the other. I see so clearly the importance of school experience in the lives of these individuals, interacting with the other variables. I cannot be content with Jencks's conclusion that the character of the school's output depends largely on a single input, namely the characteristics of the entering children. Jencks seems to be saying that the school is unimportant, and therefore that the children would do just as well if they did not go to school. I know he does not mean this, but many readers will come away from this book with just this conclusion.

If we want to understand how the various factors in the life of a child affect his development, we need to look carefully at growing children and adolescents rather than at statistical data on national samples with broad categories of cognitive skills, educational attainment, occupational status, and income. This has been done over the past four decades by many research groups, of which the Chicago group is but one.[15]

There are many places in the book where Jencks speaks favorably of schools as being generally good places for children. He also makes this point clearly in his interview with Donald Robinson published in the *Phi Delta Kappan*.[16] He is interested in making schools more "lively, comfortable, and reassuring" to children and proposes that we think of school life as an end in itself rather than a means to some other end (p. 256).

But I am not satisfied with this statement of the objective of a school as an end in itself. I think a school should be a means to the end of helping all kinds of children become competent, happy, and socially responsible adults. I am not so much interested in a school equalizing the earning powers of people, although I think greater equality of incomes is a desirable social goal.

If educators were asked to say what they want children to get out of school, I believe few would list a higher income as the principal goal. They would probably say that children should learn the three R's, some science and history, and how to be constructive citizens. They would probably say that income at a given occupational level depends on personal traits and motives that are not much influenced by schooling. In other words, few educators are likely to be interested in this book because it focuses so narrowly on adult income, which they assume depends on many factors which school does not influence.

How to Account for More of the Variance of Income

Even though I have just said that schooling should not be judged primarily on its contribution to adult incomes, I am intrigued by the data presented in the book on the general inequality of incomes among adults of the same occupational status. This inequality may be partly explained, as Levin does, by consideration of geographical differences in cost of living, and by age differences which produce differences in earning power. But there still remains so much inequality that I have tried to think about ways to account in a rational way for more of the variance of adult income, instead of relying heavily as Jencks appears to do on sheer luck as a main causal agent. I am not willing to substitute luck as a causal agent for other causes which behavioral science might discover.

Several times Jencks says that adult income must depend substantially on factors which are not measured in the usual research studies, and also on luck. That is, amount of education and IQ (level of cognitive skills) are not enough to enable us to predict who in a given occupation will be regarded as highly competent and will be rewarded accordingly. He speaks of noncognitive traits which are useful for success in certain occupations. But he confesses ignorance as to how to measure those traits, and also he gives only vague indications of what they are. Yet, if we knew what some of the traits are, and could measure them, even roughly, we would be able to understand the existing pattern of incomes, and perhaps to help some people choose their occupation so as to secure greater income.

Table 7-1 is an attempt to describe a kind of model of the relations between income, education, and a number of significant traits. It is based on the proposition that competence and reward in a given occupation are associated with amount of education, cognitive skills, and three other traits with the weights indicated. Each trait is measurable on a scale of 1 (low) to 10 (high).

For example, a successful leader in a large business or industrial establishment will score at the top of the scale on drive, well above average on IQ, will be a college graduate, but not more, will score about average on certain personality traits, and will be low in psychomotor skills. Others, less successful in this occupation, will have less optimal combinations of these characteristics.

Take the salesman as another example. The most important qualities for him are personality and drive. He does not need to be a college graduate, and he does not need more than an average IQ. The skilled craftsman who is most competent will be at the top of the scale on psychomotor skills, just about average on drive and personality, and he may be below average on IQ.

Table 7-1. Economic success, personal qualities, and amount of education:
American adult males, 1950-1970

Type of occupation	Economic level	Percent in labor force	Amount of education	Individual characteristics			
				IQ	Drive	"Personality"	Psycho-motor skills
Major business ownership and management	10	3	5	7	10	5	1
Major professional	9	3	10	8	8	6	1
College teaching	8	0.3	10	9	7	5	1
Science research	8	0.2	10	10	7	1	3
Minor business owner-manager	7	10.5	4	6	8	6	3
Artist	7	0.2	4	6	6	8	5
Minor professional	6	5	7	9	3	5	3

Technician	5	0.8	4	6	2	4	10
Salesman	7	8	4	5	8	10	1
Clerical	6	5	3	4	2	4	9
Farm owner	5	4	3	5	5	2	8
Skilled craftsman	6	20	3	2	4	4	10
Public service	4	3	3	3	4	8	4
Factory operative	3	26	2	2	1	4	9
Personal service	2	4	2	2	4	8	4
Unskilled labor	1	7	1	1	2	3	7

Definition of individual characteristics:

Amount of education—10 = Ph.D., M.D.; 8 = M.Sc.; 7 = M.A.; 5 = college graduate; 4 = some college; 3 = high school graduate;

2 = some high school; 1 = elementary school graduate

IQ = general intelligence

Drive = need achievement plus ambition

Personality = several unspecified factors

Psychomotor skills = possibly two factors

Note: The weights assigned to each of the five individual characteristics are simply estimates by the writer. They can be discovered empirically by a multivariate analysis based on measurement of a representative sample.

If we should ask a behavioral scientist to work out a reasonably good estimate of adult earnings within an occupational category among those of Table 7-1, he probably would succeed in accounting for much more of the variance than Jencks proposes. Taking the category of major business owner or manager, he would try a prediction formula something like the following:

$$\text{Income Index} = 5E + 7Q + 10D + 5P + 1S$$

where the various individual characteristics are indicated by the letters: E (amount of education); Q(IQ); D(drive); P (personality); S(physical or psychomotor skills). The traits can be measured and expressed in standard scores with a mean of 50. A business owner scoring 80 on drive and 50 on IQ would get 800 plus 350 added to his Income Index, while another person with a higher IQ(80) but a lower drive quotient(50) would get 500 plus 560 or 1060 on his Income Index, and therefore get a lower income. The researcher would work out a more sophisticated mathematical procedure, along these general lines.

In contrast to the business manager, a technician might have a predictive formula:

$$\text{Income Index} = 4E + 6Q + 2D + 4P + 10S.$$

People in this category would profit financially from a high degree of psychomotor skill, which is nearly worthless for the business manager. And they would not suffer much lowering of income due to a low drive level.

Some of these occupations are too broad to be homogeneous in their requirements. For example, a surgeon, in the major professional category, will differ substantially from a lawyer. He will need above average psychomotor skills, and can get along with somewhat less drive and personality than the lawyer.

This kind of model would not reduce the income differences between occupations, but, if it were used as a guide for vocational choice, it might reduce the variation of incomes within an occupation. And it might help to remove some of the mystery that bothers researchers on income variability.

Opportunity, Equity, and Equality

In his final chapter, "What Is to Be Done?" Jencks says: "We have seen that educational opportunities, cognitive skills, educational credentials, occupational status, income, and job satisfaction are all unequally distributed. We have not, however, been very successful in explaining most of these inequalities. The association between one variety of inequality and another is usually quite weak, which means that equalizing one thing is unlikely to have much effect on the degree of inequality in other areas. We must therefore ask whether attempts to produce equality by more direct methods would be more effective, or whether the status quo is essentially unalterable" (p. 253).

His answer is that we should use political methods to raise the incomes of the poor and reduce the incomes of the rich. We have been doing this to some degree, and I believe we should and will do it to a greater extent, especially by correcting the severe deficiencies of our welfare laws and by taxing high incomes more heavily. Jencks argues that increasing the amount of education children of low-income families or children of disadvantaged social groups receive does not result in raising their adult incomes enough to make this an important means of working for social equity. I disagree.

Jencks's methods have underestimated the effectiveness of schooling in raising incomes. Careful studies of the incomes of ethnic subgroups in relation to their education would demonstrate that amount of schooling is closely correlated with income for blacks, Chicanos, Japanese-Americans, Chinese-Americans, and for children of low-income whites. Indeed, Jencks's comments on recent developments in the incomes of black families indicate that he also inclines toward this belief.

Is it worthwhile, then, for educators to work especially hard to extend more effective education to children of low-income families? If our goal is to raise the incomes of children born into low-income and otherwise disadvantaged groups, I am convinced that more and better education for them is effective. But if our goal is to reduce the general inequality of adult incomes among the entire population, then education alone is a weak instrument.

The problem of equity. Can we have equity, or social justice, in a society with a great deal of inequality in family environments, educational opportunities, cognitive skills, educational aspirations, educational attainment, occupational status, and income? Obviously it is impossible for everyone to be equal in all these respects, nor is it necessary. But in my opinion, and in Jencks's, our society could and should reduce the inequality of incomes.

A just society is one in which people get what they want out of life, as long as their wants do not interfere with those of others. The economic wants of many people are not met as well as they should be in an affluent society, and, as citizens and as educators, we should take action to correct this situation. But people have other wants that are not closely connected with income, and these should also be met in a just society.

Education should prepare people to do their best to get what they want out of life—to develop a comfortable and satisfactory life style. If they succeed, our society will still show many inequalities, but these will be accepted and expected, and it will be a more equitable society.

This line of thinking emphasizes the importance of educational opportunity rather than educational equality. We educators will contribute more to equity by maximizing opportunity for growth and development and free choice than we will by organizing education explicitly to increase the earning power of individuals.

Conclusions

In testing or judging a society for the level of its equity, there are certain possible criteria to which we should give only a limited importance. They are equality of personal characteristics, such as cognitive skills, drive or ambition, personality, and physical skills, and equality of income. We might attempt to reduce the range of some of these, mainly by raising the lowest level.

The criteria of most value in judging the quality of a society are: life satisfaction (satisfaction with present life style and future prospects); physical and mental health; economic adequacy (efficiency in an occupation); and options available among desirable alternatives in life style.

Education should provide opportunity for the individual to enhance himself in these respects.

Notes

1. Christopher Jencks *et al.*, *Inequality: A Reassessment of the Effect of Family and Schooling in America* (New York: Basic Books, 1972).

2. *New York Times*, "Roots of Inequality," Sunday, September 10, 1972, editorial page.

3. James J. Kilpatrick, "Equality in Education Debunked," *Chicago Daily News*, September 21, 1972.

4. Daniel Bell *et al.*, "Essays on Equality," *The Public Interest* (No. 29, Fall 1972).

5. David K. Cohen, "Immigrants and the Schools," *Review of Educational Research* 40 (1970), 13-27.

6. Bayard Rustin, "Equal Opportunity and the Liberal Will," *Washington Post*, October 15, 1972, "Outlook," pp. B1, 4.

7. *Wall Street Journal*, "An Unsuitable Instrument," October 2, 1972, editorial page.

8. Henry M. Levin, "Schooling and Inequality: The Social Science Objectivity Gap," *Saturday Review/Education* 55 (No. 46, November 1972), 49-51.

9. James W. Guthrie, George B. Kleindorfer, Henry M. Levin, and Robert T. Stout, *Schools and Inequality* (Cambridge, Mass.: M.I.T. Press, 1971); Henry M. Levin, James W. Guthrie, George B. Kleindorfer, and Robert T. Stout, "School Achievement and Post-School Success: A Review," *Review of Educational Research* 41 (1971), 1-16.

10. Theodore W. Schultz (ed.), *Investment in Education: The Equity-Efficiency Quandary*, in *Journal of Political Economy* 80 (No. 3, pt. 2, May-June 1972).

11. Levin, *op. cit.*, 50.

12. *Ibid.*

13. *Ibid.*, 51.

14. Peter Blau and Otis Dudley Duncan, *The American Occupational Structure* (New York: John Wiley & Sons, 1967).

15. Daniel P. Moynihan, "The Schism in Black America," *The Public Interest* (No. 27, Spring 1972), 3-24.

16. Richard P. Coleman and Bernice L. Neugarten, *Social Status in the City* (San Francisco: Jossey-Bass, Inc., 1971); Robert J. Havighurst *et al.*, *Growing Up in River City* (New York: John Wiley & Sons, 1962); A. B. Hollingshead, *Elmtown's Youth* (New York: John Wiley & Sons, 1949); W. Lloyd Warner, Robert J. Havighurst, and Martin B. Loeb, *Who Shall Be Educated?* (New York: Harper & Bros., 1944).

17. Donald Robinson, "Interview with Christopher Jencks," *Phi Delta Kappan* 54 (December 1972), 255-57.

8. Mass Elites on the Threshold of the 1970's

Mary Jean Bowman

The decade just past has brought mass breakthroughs into the higher and more exclusive sanctuaries of the educational systems of more than one European nation, and it is evident today, on the threshold of the 1970's, that the effects have been and will be profound. Generally in Europe the impact of this thrust is felt initially at the "upper secondary" levels, which had been the gatekeepers for entry into the universities; in some countries the entire structure of secondary education has been challenged, and in a few—most notably Sweden—there have been dramatic reforms. But both secondary schools and universities have yet to experience what this rising tide can ultimately mean.

The situation in the United States has been quite different, and on two counts: first, there has been a long open-door tradition in U.S. education, and, second, the flood has reached epic proportions in the expanding colleges and universities. Despite a brief interlude in which the talk, at least, centered on quality, flooding into colleges has continued unabated. The cry widely heard now has become 'a college place for everyone!' Europeans may look with apprehension or dismay at this phenomenon, but there it is, for better or for worse.

Reprinted with permission of the Carfax Publishing Company from *Comparative Education* (Oxford, Eng.), 6 (No. 3, November 1970), 141-60.

Japan, meanwhile, falls somewhere in between, with a less firmly entrenched initial educational elitism than in Europe, with a flood into upper secondary and higher education that is unmatched outside of North America, and with a history of adaptation and readjustment of educational policies that has swung now toward some European model, now toward the United States, remaining all the while distinctively Japanese, nonetheless.

It is to the new "mass elites" of Europe and Japan that [this study] is primarily directed. How does the whole thing look to an economist—at least, to this particular economist? Where are we heading? And how far have recent events opened up or challenged thinking about the fundamental issues in social philosophy that must concern economists and educational policy makers alike? How are perceptions of recent and prospective changes related to perceptions of the nature of people and their variabilities in potentials for learning and productive life? And has the onslaught at the top submerged or diverted thought and effort about doing something for "the others" —those who have not shared in the great rush, or who are unlikely to do so in the decade ahead?

But if we are to communicate across disciplines in these important matters, it is essential first of all that the humanness of economics be better understood. There are a good many false notions floating around on this subject, notions to which economists themselves have sometimes contributed.

1. Concerning Economics and People

When I first began to teach a course in "the economics of education" a decade ago, the first thing I encountered was the assumption that the "economics of education" was the same thing as educational finance. From the educator's point of view, economics might help in getting more money for the schools. But it was also an ignoble sort of subject, concerned with such "material" matters as money and budgets—always looming up to constrain the schoolmen in their freedom of action and in the realization of some of their most luxurious (if not always their best) dreams. No one thought of economics as a discipline from which he could draw support for bigger and bigger spending on the schools.

The decade of the 1960's brought a change in that image. This was

a decade of fantastic worldwide expansion in educational establishments, both public and private. And in this explosive development
the educators found many economists to be their allies. An educated
population was needed to undergird economic growth, and who
would question that economic growth was to be desired? There must
be caveats, of course: economists' measures were just the "minimum" criteria for educational expansion. "Economic ends" were all
very well in their place, but education had its contribution to the
"higher values" as well. Economists themselves contributed to this
oversimplification of the "economic" when they let themselves get
caught up in a convenient but misleading semantics that called all the
nonmeasured returns either "noneconomic" or "social" (distinct, it
was often assumed, from "economic"). The "economic" was identified with the "monetary" when analysis was presented in monetary
terms, or with the technocratic when the "economists" were talking
about "manpower requirements." And a great deal of nonsense has
been spread around about "economic ends," when fundamentally
there is no such thing.

I would like to develop three main points here: (1) The old view
of economics as concerned with "costs," the view prevalent before
the great educational explosion of the 1960's, was in some respects
closer to a true perception of economics than the views that pervade
the more recent writings of educators, and of many planners, concerning what economics is all about. (2) The notion that somehow
economics is incapable of admitting humanistic values into its pre-
scriptions, and even that it is at loggerheads with humanism, is based
on false premises. (3) Economics is fundamentally about *people,*
which means of necessity that an analysis of how an economy works
must blend behaviorism and moral philosophy; ultimately it must do
this in a very explicit and overt fashion.

1. The first of these points comes straight to the center of what
economics is all about—the allocation of limited resources among
alternative uses. Few things in life are really "free." This is not just a
matter of money, which is only a convenient intermediary. It is
neurotic misers, not economists, who are concerned with money for
its own sake. Economics are concerned with choices among alternatives, and hence with decision making. Money wages, for example,
allow the recipient a wide range of choice among the goods and
services he can obtain in exchange for his labor. Those choices may

include, by the way, transportation to the museum, tickets to a concert, or purchase of a painting.

But this brings us to a reason why economists can be particularly annoying. For the economist cannot give license to spend and spend, indefinitely, in a "good cause"—whether what is spent is time or money. He must ask "what about the other things that could be done with some of these resources?" The reason economists were popular with many educators over the decade of the 1960's was that, taking as a criterion contributions to measured national income or its growth, they had come up with "objective" assessments that suggested further investments in schooling to be a favorable alternative to other uses of resources.[1] The 1970's can bring quite different assessments.

Another question the economist has conventionally asked in looking at education has been: "Couldn't you accomplish the same things (whatever they may be) at less cost?" Make your ends as humanistic or "spiritual" as you wish, something is always foregone in the utilization of staff and student time and the provision of more rather than less elegant facilities. If the economist is more than a blown up bookkeeper, he will emphasize that the "cost" of anything *is* the alternative foregone when resources are used (or wasted) on the one activity. Money estimates of costs are then meaningful only as they constitute reasonably good surrogates for the foregone alternatives. *All real costs are opportunity costs.* It is no accident that, as economists dug in to examine education more intensively during the 1960's, costs in this generic meaning were made more visible and even measured. For a time even the attempt at such measurement evoked considerable controversy, details of how to do it aside. It was argued, for example, that to count foregone earnings of students as a cost was not legitimate because those figures were "not included in the national accounts!" This is about as clear an example as one could ask of the dangers of letting bookkeepers' conventions prevail over thought, forgetting that the basic problem is choosing among alternatives. But readers interested in these debates about "foregone earnings" of students can pursue them elsewhere.[2]

To educators, one of the more interesting implications of the economist's way of thinking must be with respect to the use of student time even among pupils too young to participate in the labor force. Pupil time is inherently limited, and hence costly. When a child spends an hour on mathematics, for example, he is giving up an hour of something else; the alternative might be music, or French language, or play—as you will. The opportunity-cost of his last (marginal) hour in mathematics is the value, however assessed, of his best foregone use of that hour. There is nothing in the economist's logic to suggest that the best use of the hour may not be play; indeed, this must sometimes be the case. The difficulty, of course, is that we have no handy surrogate measure (like money) for valuing these alternatives. The economist has underlined a problem that calls for continuous re-examination as educators reassess the functioning of the schools; but in stressing this problem the economist has not resolved it. In this example he could rarely go beyond asking some of the right questions (which, by the way, is sometimes more important than giving "answers"). However, conventional "cost-effectiveness" analysis is possible wherever we can put price tags of some sort on the resources used in alternative programs, whatever the goals of those programs may be.

2. I have already indicated sufficiently that economics does not preclude the inclusion of humanistic values in its decision models, even though "values" and personal "satisfactions" cannot be measured directly. Also, it should be clear that monetary gain is not viewed in economics as an end *in itself.* Here I want to direct attention to a paradox: the most striking example of a nonhumanistic or even antihumanistic activity in economics may be found precisely in some of the literature on educational and manpower planning—not in monetary theory or in business-enterprise research. I refer to the technocratic approaches to "manpower planning," whereby two-legged skills are moved about on the drawing boards in accordance with "manpower requirements," which in turn are supposed to be "functional" even if not in accord with the ways in which men prefer to balance pay against satisfactions in their job and career decisions. It is not that the men who engage in that type of "manpower planning" are inhuman. Indeed, again and again they will insist on the importance of taking into account also the "social demands" for education, and they mean it. At the same time, however, they are setting up an illusory distinction that identifies all except "manpower requirements" considerations as noneconomic or even "dysfunctional." And if we were to take what they write seriously, it would seem that the one thing they most deplore is the man who prefers to

earn less and enjoy his work at his own expense. This technocratic
view feeds into, even as it also reflects, a tendency—most extreme in
France but widespread in Europe—to draw a dichotomy between the
"technological" and the "humanistic."[3]

This view is shallow economically because in the technocratic approach the fundamental question of the meaning of "national income" is totally evaded, and with this evasion any estimated "manpower requirements" lack a philosophical base. There is no social
criterion: no analysis of whose is the power, whose the wisdom,
whose the judgments whereby the society is to be made to "function."

Use of technology is by no means the same thing as technocratic
manpower planning, however, and I am not contending that technology is contrahumanist. The problem in this respect, and it is a
serious one, is in the ways in which old-style "humanists," and
among them many educators, view technology. W. D. Halls[4] puts this
far better than I could, and for making such a statement he has far
better credentials:

The theorists and practitioners of technology, such as M. Capelle, have not so far
succeeded in convincing those undergoing education, nor the educators themselves, that technology is in fact part of a new humanism. Yet it *is* a humanism
because it liberates men from ignorance, takes away the drudgery from their
work, and allows them to enjoy their leisure more profitably. Furthermore—and
this point has not yet been seized at all—technology demands a combination of
mental and manual skills that makes nonsense of the separation of those that
work with their head and those that work with their hands—surely one of the
most destructive forms of social cleavage ever conceived by man.

This "cleavage" of which Halls speaks is outside of economics; nor
does it set the economic apart from the noneconomic. But the related, false cleavage that separates "manpower requirements" out as
"the economic" function of education may be almost as damaging so
far as educational policy formation is concerned. The proclivity in
some quarters to treat "social" and "economic" demands for education as polar concepts, and then to argue that one or the other must
be accorded "priority," must be one of the most naively irrespon-
sible bits of nonsense currently perpetrated in the intellectual world.

3. To suppose that economics could exist divorced from an ultimate concern with people is to conceive of economics as very different from the field of learning to which a long line of great men have

contributed, from Adam Smith right up to the present day. There can be technicians who ignore the people behind their data, or esoteric theorists whose interests are in a purely mathematical game, to be sure, and these men do make important contributions to economics; but economics is not statistics. Economics is and must be concerned ultimately with the behavior of people and with a study of the interaction processes by which an "economy" operates. It must necessarily, then, be concerned with moral philosophy. But this is also why in the final analysis there is no such thing as an "economic end." Nevertheless, evaluative criteria relating to the functioning of the economic system play a particularly important part in economics in two ways: they define the broad problems to which economists direct their major efforts, and the criteria themselves become more adequately specified as they re-emerge in the progress of theoretical and empirical research into the functioning of economic systems.

I have been impressed recently by the close parallel between the major concerns expressed by leading noneconomists concerned with problems and policies in education and the key concerns of economists. At a recent conference on secondary education and its development over the past decade in four European countries, the papers included emphasis in varying degrees on (a) "economic requirements," (b) "democratization," or "equal opportunity," and (c) "freedom of choice." Frequently the last of these was seen as in conflict with the first, and both (b) and (c) were commonly perceived as noneconomic. Since these are precisely the kinds of questions that an economist must ask, I have been astounded to discover that many people think that the idea of freedom of choice is somehow "sociological" rather than "economic." That conclusion denies the whole stream of developments in neoclassical economics from Jeremy Bentham right up to the present day, and among "marginalists" and "antimarginalists," alike. How, I ask you, could anyone analyze the functioning of an economic system without considering the system of incentives whereby men are induced to invest their resources, human and otherwise, in productive activities that are in line with wants of other men? How could we pretend to analyze the functioning of a system without considering the processes by which it allocates both opportunities to produce and to consume—including opportunities to invest in capacities to produce and to enjoy leisure?

Some economists may for a time concentrate their efforts on national-income accounting and on "economic growth" as an aggregate of sorts, but in the end they must come back to examining the operations of the system and the *shape* of growth. Economists must come back always to what economics is all about—to what, in the new vocabulary, is "relevant." It is important to listen to the new "radical economists," not because what they say is new, or because in its specifics it is right (or wrong), but because they are searching for human meanings. This has nothing to do with being Marxist or anti-Marxist.[5]

2. Concerning Mass Elites, Social Goals, and the Nature of Man

In 1950-51 the certificated leavers from upper-secondary education taken as a proportion of the relevant age group ranged between 3 and 9 percent in the countries of northern Europe—except Finland, which had reached 23 percent. This was close to the Japanese figure of 27 percent. The United States already had well over half (59 percent) of its youth graduating from high school. Granted that completion of upper-secondary school did not mean the same thing across countries, these figures nevertheless indicate the general order of differences in proportions with potential access to college. Fifteen years later there was a much greater diversity. Austria, Denmark, Germany, the Netherlands and the United Kingdom were still graduating less than 10 percent of the age cohort from the last stage of upper-secondary school; France and Sweden had reached 13 and 14 percent, respectively; Belgium and Norway were at 19, and Ireland was at 24 percent. Finland and Japan meanwhile were crowding the 50 percent mark, and in the United States three-fourths of the age group were completing this level of schooling. The Japanese figure has since climbed to very nearly the 1965 U.S. level.[6]

To a North American, the European figures still look small—with the exception of the Finnish and the impressive performance in Ireland relative to income levels in that country. Nevertheless, the expansion of secondary attendance seems impressive indeed to many Europeans, who see in these developments the portents of a revolution in the basis upon which their traditional upper-secondary and university systems have been built.

One impact, in some ways a minor one, has been a retreat from "manpower requirements forecasting" and manpower planning, although one finds the forces being gathered again when discussions turn to types of curricula in either secondary or higher education. In the words of OECD's Committee on Scientific and Technical Personnel:[7] "The evolution of the Committee's work reflects the trend away from primarily economic preoccupations to the more general social aspect of adapting secondary education to increased participation and reconciling this shift with the needs of a complex society." I am not sure whether the writers intend to imply that in practice manpower planning once had an effect but has no more, or whether they are talking of what "ought" to have been or to be, or whether, finally, they are simply bowing to the inevitable. In any case, their retreat is not only from manpower planning but from any sort of economic analysis or economic assessment at all—for they make no attempt to recast their economic thinking.

It is clear, at the same time, that the recent changes and their implications for the future are perceived to be of a major order of importance. Thus we have the following statements:[8] "It is this mass participation which makes necessary the formulation of new objectives, new course content and new criteria for pupil evaluation. Increased demand does not mean simply providing more places, but calls for a reconsideration of the concept of secondary education." Or again, two pages later, we read that: "Unless the structure, the content and the criteria of evaluating the present secondary systems are suitably adapted, mass participation and equal opportunities cannot be attained." Just how difficult the very idea of "equal opportunity" may be, let alone its implementation in the present European context, is indicated by a remark at the bottom of the same page: "In addition, any changes at this level are limited by demand on the part of the principal consumer of secondary school graduates, namely higher education." The strong tone of traditional elitism that runs through these passages is evident, along with simultaneous protestations of concern for "democratic processes" and "equalization of opportunity"—whether or not for "freedom of choice." The problem of how curricula should be reorganized, supplemented, or adapted for the larger and more diverse participation in secondary schools is fundamental, on both efficiency (learning effectiveness) and equity grounds:[9]

It was the combined need to create (a) a system adapted to mass participation and (b) conditions for full educational opportunity, that called for a revision of secondary education structure. The fact that the young people for whom the syllabuses of selective general secondary schools had traditionally been prepared were now outnumbered by those with a different social background made more obvious the strong bias which the curricula, teaching methods and ultimately, the built-in value systems which the different types of school had acquired over the years. Such social and cultural biases as these proved to be obstacles to the successful integration of large numbers of the new types of children, particularly into "academic" general secondary schools. They also hindered the setting up of a more flexible structural relationship between parallel types of secondary schooling, and the easy transfer between the various programmes. This was particularly true of the many countries where, until very recently, a selective secondary educational system co-existed with one of compulsory primary education. . . . The system of two parallel courses, one academic and selective catering for the needs of a social and/or an intellectual elite, the other terminal—providing either a general or a technical-vocational programme—catering for a larger group of presumably lower intellectual standard and social class, becomes increasingly inadequate in view of the educational objective of full opportunity for all available talent.

As I look at the various passages quoted, and at similar discussions elsewhere, I am struck by the extent to which the thinking and the planning for secondary education seems to be appearing as an adaptive adjustment *after* the event rather than leading events—although there are important exceptions (for example, in Sweden). This position was indeed taken quite explicitly with respect to higher education in the report of the OECD conference on Higher Education, as the following quotations make clear:[10]

The first point brought home to the participants was that in most member countries the realization of the need to adapt the structures of higher education is not generally the result of any rethinking by the Universities themselves. It clearly comes from outside, under the pressure of the spontaneous demand for places by students and the need for qualified personnel to meet the requirements of economic expansion. The compelling necessity for re-adjustment obviously makes it more difficult and more urgent to seek solutions and put them into effect. . . . No less decisive is the fact that a growing proportion of the population now considers a university course as the key to a successful social and professional career. As Prof. Weil pointed out, access to higher education is increasingly regarded by public opinion as a right which it seems difficult to restrict without repudiating democratic ideals in education.

And so men want to be democratic and elitist at the same time. They are further harassed by the obstacle that you could not make people "equal" even if you really wanted to. Writers have become increasingly aware—how could they help it—of rising popular demands for places in secondary schools and universities, especially in the elite-type secondary streams. But rarely if ever does an educator, and in continental Europe even an economist, pay any attention to decision theory at all. Hence little thought is given to exploring possibilities for maximizing the social efficiency of individual self-selection into one or another type of schooling and occupational career. For much the same reason, plus some mistaken or superficial notions about "economic democracy" and "freedom of choice," there is a common disregard of the effects of who pays for what. And, understandably, few perceive the nature of "manpower planning" as a psycho-social phenomenon in the world of the intelligentsia.

Among other misconceptions that pervade large parts of the literature are the treatments of "general" education as if it were noneconomic or nonvocational. There are exceptions, however. For example, Dr. Halls, in a paper I cited earlier, stresses that the common "general" school is at once democratic and economically viable; it is there that young people get their initial grounding in the basic learning-to-learn, or communication subjects. Ordinary people often demonstrate a greater appreciation of this fact than the "experts." With respect to upper-secondary levels, there is a prevalent tendency to confound the "general" with the "gentlemanly," which may be quite nongeneral in terms of learning to learn, the really critical requirement for effective participation in a dynamic economy. The tendency to hang upper-secondary schools on the universities is of course tied in with this set of perceptions, perhaps most notably in England. In many instances (and this does not exclude the United States) an outmoded intellectual elitism seems to be quite incapable of understanding the new humanistic challenges that young people are bringing before us. Youth have not provided the answers, of course, but if their search for "relevance" is as yet rather fumbling, it is not any less important on that account. Though he puts it in quite another way, Edmund King summed up the gist of these last remarks very tidily when he said, "technology and social changes logically imply a different order of esteem for skills and types of knowledge, as well as a more pluralistic approach to private and social relevance."[11] This is indeed a time when men are challenged to creative thinking and experimentation. It is a time when the thinkable and the doable are extraordinarily open and diverse. But also, I fear, in some important respects the time may be short, and some of the critical decisions (whether made overtly or by default) may prove nonreversible.

3. From Schools to Jobs, Then and Now

What has happened, and what will happen to youth who go through various levels and kinds of schools as they enter the labor market? What about the recent and prospective effects of the mass thrust to higher levels of schooling on those who remain behind? How are these matters perceived and what are some of the clues that may help us? Such are the questions I wish to touch upon in this section.

Decent Jobs and the Crystal Balls

It is almost a quarter of a century now since Seymour Harris, in a book called *The Market for College Graduates,*[12] warned of an imminent oversupply of such graduates in the United States, with thousands of frustrated young people unable to find "suitable" jobs. In the event, college enrollments rose even more than Harris had anticipated, but so did demands for the graduates: over the course of two decades, at least, the predicted day of reckoning did not come. Ten years ago a well-known Swedish economist argued before a seminar at the University of Chicago that any expansion in the Swedish upper-secondary schools would mean a glut of educated people. Nevertheless, the Swedish school reform went through, and thus far I have not heard of unmanageable surpluses of trained people in Sweden. As a matter of fact, Swedish university graduates are probably the most occupationally selective in the world. So far, in brief, predictions of doom have not been fulfilled in either Western Europe or the United States. Neither have they been fulfilled in Japan—if, indeed, such predictions were made there—although there has been a continuous bemoaning of the assumed deterioration in quality of higher education in that country. The crystal balls were badly clouded, it would seem. But the fact that the increased numbers who came out of the secondary schools and the universities during the

1960's found at least reasonably receptive job markets does not in itself imply that this will be the experience of the 1970's as well.

Today the voices that would warn us against training too many youth seem to be rising once again, both in numbers and in volume. Is it not time to sit down and take count of stock? From the side of the manpower planners we are hearing now about the dangers of both under- and over-supply. And with this are the debates as to "which is worse"—a planner's error that produces too many or too few of one or another sort of high-level manpower? We are hearing again about the threats of overeducation from the unregenerate (even if sometimes unconscious) elitists, who fear that this time there will indeed not be the "suitable" jobs. And related, but nevertheless quite different, is the concern that young people may be making current educational decisions with false perceptions about what those decisions will mean for the future. Thus, in a summary report of the conference on higher education sponsored by OECD in 1969, we read:[13]

Nevertheless, nobody believes that institutions of higher education can continue to disregard the question of their graduates' prospects. In future they will have to co-operate with the employment services in briefing students as to the careers open to them. A student's freedom of choice is indeed purely theoretical in the absence of any briefing policy.

What can we say about these matters? First of all it is necessary to specify more precisely the question and the criteria from which we start. The most fruitless and backward-looking criterion is surely the notion of a "suitable job." The illogicality of combining the "suitable job" idea with democratic goals must be obvious. The whole idea of "suitable" or, as it is often phrased by today's students, "decent" jobs is inherently an elitist notion.[14] The ultimate nonsense in this mode of thinking is illustrated by French students who were calling for a free university system open to all, and to all who passed through the universities the guarantee of "suitable" jobs. I have encountered the same thing among a few students in the United States. If a "decent" job is defined in such a way that only 20 percent of the entry jobs in a society are "decent," it would be a bit difficult to ensure, for example, that half to three-fourths of an age cohort coming out of U.S. colleges in the future could find "decent" entry jobs.

How extremely diverse are conceptions of a decent or suitable job in fact, and how closely conditioned by actual experience, is easily illustrated by looking at occupation-education associations across nations. The extremes are probably Sweden and Japan. Just one or two occupations are enough to make the point. In Sweden the 1960 proportion of university graduates in clerical occupations was 1.5 percent and the proportion in sales occupations was 2.5 percent.[15] In Japan the proportion of university graduates who were in clerical employments was 43 percent in 1957 and 31 percent in 1967; the proportions in sales employment had meanwhile risen from 6 to 19 percent.[16] The corresponding figures for the United States in 1960 were 9 percent clerical and 9 percent sales.[17] Granted that the Swedish university graduate is typically more highly trained than the Japanese (or than university men in most other countries), this contrast remains an impressive one. It is all the more significant when one considers that the upper-secondary schools of Sweden have been so highly selective and perform to such an extent the function of grooming students for university places.

Counting the Monetary Costs and Benefits

Given the diversities in occupational patterns associated with levels and kinds of education in one country compared to another, it is evident enough that neither an elitist "suitability" criterion nor a notion of "fit" in the manpower-planning sense is going to get us very far toward understanding what has happened and what may happen in the markets for graduates of secondary schools and universities. Another way of looking at the markets for graduates of the various levels of education, much more satisfactory to most economists, is to examine the heights and shapes of the streams of life earnings that are associated with varying amounts of prior schooling. Here I shall skip that step, however, to go directly to measures that indicate just how good an investment each increment of schooling may seem to be as measured in money terms. For this purpose I shall use some rate-of-return estimates, but with a warning that such measures can be extremely tricky and must be interpreted with great caution.

It is only this year that anyone has attempted to codify the assorted evidence concerning rates of return to investments in schooling for various countries of Europe.[18] For the U.S. the decennial census (along with sample censuses taken in intervening years) permits us to go back to 1939 with roughly, though not completely comparable, data. For Japan we have fully comparable figures for large samples of workers (in firms employing ten or more persons) at intervals since 1954. Combining these with other data for Japan, I have estimated private rates of return for the years 1954, 1961, and 1966 in that country along with social rates for 1961 (Table 8-1). The rows labeled "no net direct costs" make the simplifying assumption that earnings (or scholarships) during the schooling period match any direct costs to individuals in tuition payments, fees, and so on. The 1961 "low" and "high" direct-cost estimates in the upper half of the table and the distinction between national and private institutions in the lower half were introduced because there is a very important difference between the public and private institutions so far as costs to individuals are concerned. This is in fact a matter that is being widely discussed in Japan at the present time. (It would have been better had data permitted adjustments for bonuses in all years, but I was able to do this for 1961 only.) The third column refers to *ronin*, who take examinations over again before gaining access to the university. Some take such examinations two, three, or even more times. However, the assumption in column (3) is one year as a ronin, during which period earnings are zero; being a ronin of course lowers the rates of return. However, for a particular individual it could pay off if thereby he gains access to a public university, since he will then escape the very high tuition charges and fees he would have to pay at a private university of comparable quality and prestige.

The most striking feature of this table is the marked decline in private rates of return to investment in university and junior college education suggested by a comparison of the 1954 and the 1961 estimates. There are several important reasons for this change. (a) There were substantial increases in proportions of the labor force with university education. (b) Significant changes have occurred in the structure of Japanese labor markets within less than a decade. And (c) there has been a shift in characteristics of workers who had completed "junior college" or its presumed equivalent. In 1954 a major fraction of the male "junior college" graduates who were in their prime earning years had attended higher technical institutes of the prewar period; many of these men were in high-level technical positions. By 1961 that group was old enough that their earnings had less effect in estimates of internal rates of return based on cross-section age-income data. By 1966, the older cohorts of junior college men were fading away. The high private marginal internal rate of return to university over junior college indicated by the 1966 data of column (5) is attributable mainly to the reduced relative earnings of the remaining postwar, junior college men, in lesser part to the high Japanese growth rate. Much more reliable as indicators of what has happened with respect to investments in full university education are the estimates provided in columns (2) and (3).

At no time did investments in upper-secondary education (column 1) promise really high rates of return; furthermore, the private rates shown suggest that returns to such investment have been declining. But the rate for 1966 is almost certainly biased downward because it is based on a comparison that includes older cohorts of lower-secondary or upper-primary graduates who were more often the beneficiaries of substantial on-the-job learning and training than youth with only compulsory schooling can expect in the future.

In computing the "social" rates of return (shown for 1961 in the lower half of the table), I counted all direct costs of providing educational services, whether covered by tuition payments and fees or not. There is no adjustment for scholarships, since they are transfer payments and not real resource indicators. (The value of foregone earnings of students is automatically taken into account in the comparison with the life earnings for those at the next lower level on the educational scale.) In general the estimates based on the 1961 cross-section relationships give very low social rates of return for university as well as for secondary education; it is of course at the university level and for those attending the national institutions that the discrepancy between private and social rates of return is greatest.

To put these Japanese figures in better perspective, it may be helpful to compare them with data for other countries. Generally, such estimates as exist show social rates of return in Europe to be of very nearly the same order of magnitude as those for Japan (although the samples are poor and the estimates are far from reliable). Estimates for Great Britain as of 1964, the most nearly comparable with the figures for Japan in methods of estimation, are higher than the Japanese for O-level secondary school completion (an estimated social rate of 12.5), though the British university figures are close to those for the Japanese national schools—of the university level. Analagous social rates for the United States as of 1949 ran at approximately 11 percent and 10 percent for secondary schools and

Table 8-1. Internal rates of return to education in Japan

		School interval			
		Four-year university			
Private rates of return	Upper secondary	Without ronin	One-year ronin	Junior college	Last two years of university
Income estimates without bonus adjustments:					
(a) No net direct costs					
1954	8	19	12	18	21
1961	7	10	8	11	9
1966	5	13	10	9	22
(b) Low direct cost					
1961	6	9	8	11	8
(c) High direct cost					
1961	6	8	7	10	6
Income estimates with bonus adjustments:					
(a) No net direct costs					
1961	9	12	10	12	12
(b) Low direct costs					
1961	8	10	9	10	10
(c) High direct costs					
1961	8	9	7	9	9

Social Rates of Return, 1961

Income estimates without bonus adjustments:					
National institutions	5	5	3	9	2
Private institutions	5	7	6	10	5
Income estimates with bonus adjustments:					
National institutions	7	6	5	9	4
Private institutions	7	9	8	10	9

Note: The sample refers to employees in establishments with ten or more workers. Service industries and government employment are not included. Real estate, finance, and utilities are included.

colleges respectively (taking the full four-year sequences in each case). However, by 1960 the rate for white males at the secondary school level had risen substantially in the United States. (For the college level, U.S. rates changed very little over the decade.) This reflects a phenomenon still very distant indeed so far as Europe is concerned—an increasing spread between the earnings of the large majority of the younger cohorts who complete secondary school, and earnings of the shrinking minority of disadvantaged subpopulations (white or black) and of negatively selected individuals who fail to do so. It is significant that this effect does not show up in the Japanese figures for returns to completion of secondary education.

One of the most impressive distinctions between the Japanese and other situations is the extraordinary retention rates for masses of students who enter the upper-secondary schools. Taking, for example, the cohort who entered those schools in 1963, I estimated that only 3 or 4 percent of the males and hardly more of the females dropped out; such a record would be impossible if the practice were to hold students back until they reached some specified (relatively high) level of performance;[19] but the pursuance of a regular promotion policy (also found widely in the United States) obviously is not in itself enough to account for this amazing performance. At the same time, the Japanese data indicate that mass participation in secondary education (to an extent as yet unimagined in Europe, if we except Finland) does not *necessarily* entail high dropout rates, as has so often been asserted or feared. What creates dropouts and discourages continuation in school is a very complex matter—excepting, of course, the tautological creation of "dropouts" by definition or redefinition of completion norms. Even granting that the measured private returns to investment in upper-secondary education in Japan are probably biased downward (because of shifting cohort effects), there can be no denying the strong Japanese commitment to education all along the line. This shows up despite relatively modest monetary returns to both secondary and higher education and despite modest expectations with respect to job opportunities as compared with college graduates elsewhere—even in the United States.

The Paths from Secondary School

When they leave the upper-secondary schools, what paths will young people take? Shall those paths lead to ivied walls, to red brick, or out into the world of work? Shall they follow short routes or long ones? Shall the paths be laid out with tidy borders that set them clearly apart, and with traffic carefully controlled to avoid over-crowding at the checking points? Or shall the paths be interlacing, ill-defined, and even unkempt? When, if ever, is the human product really finished? And how smoothly will the new cohorts coming out of the secondary schools ride the waves of the future? On these questions, which could occupy us for hundreds of pages, I shall make only a few observations—with special comments, again, concerning Japan.

(1) First, there can hardly be any doubt that it is the Europeans who lean most strongly toward the "neatly-hedged" pattern; the North Americans tolerate more untidiness. Associated with this are quite different ways in which scholars or planners view direct labor-market entry versus continuation into universities on the part of graduates of the senior secondary schools. No one could doubt, for example, that the last sentence, at least, of the following comment came from a European:[20]

On the whole, the labour market has easily absorbed the increased number of secondary leavers from technical and commercial schools, though their training and the numbers trained in particular fields did not always correspond to the immediate needs. . . . The increase in the number of potential candidates for higher education has, on the contrary, been much less easily absorbed and has in many countries led to acute problems of accommodation.

The main worry expressed in these quotations is that youth trained in general academic schools may not find the university places that will allow them to continue in academically selective paths. As I see it, there are only two logically possible interpretations of such a statement, either or both of which might apply. As with the idea of "suitable jobs," either this anxiety basically expresses intellectual elitism, or it derives from fixed-coefficient manpower thinking. If the latter, does this then mean that academic secondary pupils are con-sidered to be ill-equipped for work unless they go on to universities? If so, the "general" curricula are very far from general—a matter about which we commented earlier.

At the other extreme, to the untidy rather than the tidy side, educators from the United States would usually look upon any al-leged "excess" of secondary graduates *seeking* university places as evidence of a failure to keep the educational system really open. Many, if not most, would assume as a matter of course that the places would just have to be found or made. Excepting for a few specialities (notably medicine) it is taken for granted that student demands rather than "places" will determine enrollments, and not only in higher education at large but also among curricula.[21] If the U.S. high school graduate wants to continue in school but cannot get into one institution, he can usually get into another.

Japan partakes in some degree of both worlds, though for the moment the actual situation is closer to the North American than the European. An overriding fact is Japan's massive, unrestrained appetite for more and more schooling for everyone, even as, at the same time, there is a manifest pull back toward more traditional specialization among the secondary schools and toward a differentiation of higher education by types, levels and functions more nearly in the prewar pattern. The pull and tug between intellectual elitism and democratic goals, evidenced almost everywhere, manifest themselves in Japan in ways that are quite distinctive from the European. In part this reflects the effects of two decades of experience with a school structure that was reshaped during the American occupation, but more fundamental is the old and pervasive value placed on education in Japan.

Thus we have today serious discussions about making education compulsory through the senior-secondary years—now that 70 percent or more of a cohort is already completing that level.[22] But at the same time we read that it is necessary to study how best the contents and methods of education may be adapted to develop "the different characteristics of men and women."[23] There is widespread pressure from many Japanese educators in favor of more separate vocational-technical schools, but at the same time it is specified that there should be opportunities to take vocational subjects along with a general course—"in view of the fact that about 40 percent of graduates from the general course (are) taking jobs."[24] Or again, importance is placed on university training by the big modern firms when recruiting the young people on whose talents they want to build. But it is pointed out also that recently "some large-scale enterprises recruit . . . upper secondary school graduates rather than university graduates whose quality has lowered on the average."[25] Where else in the world could such a collection of pieces be put together? Here we have the pragmatic, adaptive, imitative if you will, but withal the profoundly and unquestionably Japanese.

(2) However broad the paths and however open the system with respect to selectivity into one sort of curriculum or another, into higher education, or into the labor market, in Japan there may still be narrow and clearly marked paths into select universities—the greatest of the imperial universities of Japan. And there may be equally narrow routes from these universities into what the Japanese sometimes call "super-express careers" in private industry or in the national bureaucracy. Even in the United States there is unquestionably university selectivity into careers at the top, though on a comparative scale the U.S. pattern is an open one. In England few would question the reality of the gentlemanly tradition in the placing of graduates of Oxford and Cambridge. But again I would like to draw attention especially to Japan.

The situation in Japan is one that has given members of the Central Council for Education grave concern, for they observe that the ramifications, from both efficiency and "equal opportunity" points of view are many and complex:[26]

The current tendency of leading employers opening the door of employment only to the graduates of certain specific universities not only obstructs the equal opportunity of employment but also makes a key factor responsible for the inflexible social appraisal of universities and the intensified competition for admission into a group of universities.

The themes packed into this compact statement are reiterated on page after page of the *Interim Report,* but especially with reference to criteria of labor market placement by ability or merit rather than clique affiliations, and with reference to the ronin problem and its aggravation. The latter problem is a major one; in recent years approximately a third of the successful applicants to universities have had one or more years as ronin, and among males entering the junior colleges the 1967 figure was 40 percent.[27] These high rates explain what might otherwise surprise the uninitiated, the very high "unemployment" rates among graduates of senior-secondary schools as compared with youth entering the labor market at completion of the nine years of compulsory schooling.

(3) Educators from Europe and the United States alike frequently reveal a decided bias toward schools, of whatever kind, as the places

where learning must occur. Experience counts, to be sure, but the Western educator who will stress the importance of learning on the job for any except the less schooled must be rare indeed. Quite contrary to what is often supposed, learning on the job is an extremely important part of the formation of human productive capacities. Indeed, one of the things that makes analysis of "human capital" so difficult, and sometimes elusive, is that one can never quite know when it is "done." The Japanese may protest that they provide very little training at work, but this is by way of apology. They display an awareness of the indefinite extension of human learning that will not be matched in Europe or America. And this fact mediates the seemingly "poor" occupational status for university graduates suggested by the statistics cited earlier. For the important thing is unquestionably the "career express" the young man manages to board. When asked his present job or occupation, the educated Japanese youth is very likely to respond instead with a statement about for whom he works. This is not solely on account of the "life commitment system," but there is an evident enough connection. Summarizing a complex and much-discussed institution in the simplest possible terms, the "life commitment system" of today entails a greater commitment on the part of the employer than of the employee; it is an exaggerated sort of seniority system. An understanding of this institution is essential if we are to understand how schooling and work are related over the life span in Japan; but that is not all. Simply because the seniority system is more conspicuous in Japan, we may discover things there that are equally relevant and could serve similar functions in other countries. Both the adherent of "rate-of-return" analysis and the manpower requirements forecaster must do a bit of juggling to take in the situation in Japan. When the big firm has men on its hands up to retirement age and is committed not only to pay them but to keep them busy at work that will not too blatantly offend their dignity, it has a very direct interest in making sure that obsolescence does not hit too hard or too soon. There is no danger of falling into the trap of identifying skill packages with men.

4. Concerning Freedom of Choice, Democracy and Opportunity

Many people today would accept quite casually, and without question, the notion that if you make something free (like higher education) you enlarge the scope for "freedom of choice." I shall contend that this is a major fallacy. I shall then go on to argue that two of the educational policies frequently urged in the name of democratization or equalization of educational opportunity are in fact antidemocratic under most circumstances.

(1) *"Social Demand" is a private affair.* Or such is the case, at any rate, in the current jargon of many educational and manpower planners. It is a private affair in that it is what individuals faced with certain alternatives will seek educationally—at which doors how many of them will knock. Interpreted in this way, "social demand" will be as "private" with a centrally planned and controlled educational system as with a system that is open and flexible. But the extent to which the private demand so defined is realized, and what such a "demand" means with respect to freedom of choice is another matter. Let us set aside the question as to how informed people are in making their choices, agreeing that provision of information is both desirable and difficult.

Even if they are *informed* as to the external effects of their decisions, will people be *wise*; will they correctly assess what is in their self-interest and act accordingly? Do we, the elect (whether or not the elected), stand ready to impose our judgments upon and over theirs? Unquestionably just such an evaluation has been one of the reasons (though not the sole one) for legislating compulsory education. But carrying this argument up to higher levels in the educational system poses some very awkward questions. I shall let this dilemma pass, noting only that even were we the possessors of superior wisdom (which personally I doubt), that superiority would not necessarily be contraindicative of the value of freedom of choice. There is something to be said for allowing men to make their own errors. And in any case, what we are talking about here is how far the value of "freedom of choice" is approximated and what, specifically, we mean by it.

A second and crucial question is of course *whose* freedom of choice? Does it make a difference whether the people doing the choosing are rich or poor, intelligent or dull, from families that contribute to their learning in the home or families that have been unable to do so, and so forth? How can "freedom of choice" be separated, as a value, from "equalization of opportunity"? The answer must be that ultimately it cannot. For the moment, however, I defer examination of the distribution of ability to pay. We will come back to it after we sort out the allocative question of expressions of preferences within any given distributional context.

This brings us to the central question, or cluster of questions, that must be specified in analyzing how far educational policies in fact support the free expression of preferences, how far they may distort them. Or to put this in another way, we may ask how far those policies induce individuals to express their preferences in ways that accord with the social interest? Some examples will help. Suppose an educational system in which all candidates qualifying for entrance to the university may secure places tuition-free. What will this imply? Evidently "social demand" as that term is used in the manpower-planning literature will be fully realized, neither more nor less. However, because tuition is free, some qualified individuals will choose to go to the university who, had they been provided the same sum of money to use for whatever purpose they preferred, would have made quite another choice. By making tuition free instead of charging fees to match the costs of the educational services, the policy makers have distorted the signals instead of leaving expression of preferences to the individuals concerned. This may be justified on some other grounds, but free tuition is *not* compatible with full freedom of choice!

Or is it? We can, and indeed must, qualify this negative conclusion provided the extra benefits accruing to third parties (i.e., the general public) *over and above* benefits received from his education by the individual are approximated by the tuition subsidies. The greater the direct costs for which tuition subsidies are provided, the greater will be the distortion and the interference with real freedom of choice unless the third-party or "external" benefits are equally big. With the increasing tendency in many countries to provide not only tuition but also subsistence allowances for university students, the situation becomes yet more exaggerated. It is far more difficult than most intellectuals like to believe to make a good case for larger externalities at the higher levels of the educational system.

It is hardly surprising that more people should choose to spend time in university life when subsidized to do so, or that heavy subsidies to students in public universities should discourage the development of private facilities even when there is crowding at the doors of the public institutions. The really remarkable thing is to be observed, again, in Japan. There, despite the very substantial gap between costs to the individual in the public and in the private institutions, even the latter receive many thousands of students. There are distortions within the system, as the ronin attest, but demand *even at full cost* is impressive.

In launching this discussion of distortions of free choice I "supposed" not that *all* candidates for university entrance would get in, but that this was true of all *qualified* candidates. Setting qualification constraints is one way of limiting numbers even when tuition is free and those admitted receive subsistence grants. But so far as freedom to choose is concerned, this is obviously no substitute for charging full-cost tuition as a signal of true costs. On the contrary, youth who cannot "qualify" do not have the university option *at any price.* If we assume free tuition, those who can qualify have still the distorted set of options that subsidized tuition entails. What, then, are the grounds for using control by qualifications? I suggest that one or more of three underlying attitudes or perceptions are entailed. One notion, very flattering to the intellectual but dubious on moral grounds, is that people born with brains are somehow nobler, or "more deserving" of special rewards. This is intellectual elitism in its most arrogant form. The second is a belief that the more able will benefit more from additional schooling *and* that individuals in making their choices will not allow adequately for that fact; this is a special version of the "superior wisdom" theme noted earlier. Third, it could be argued that the external benefits are especially great from educating the most able individuals. Only the third of these arguments, I submit, has even a whisper of empirical and moral validity.

To me, the strangest view of all is that when young people knowingly make not only educational but also occupational choices contrary to the specifications of manpower requirements analysis this is somehow "dys-economic." It is a wonder that such an argument did not collapse in ashes long ago. But I have said enough of this earlier.

(2) *Affluent parents are a problem.* In fact they are a double problem, with respect both to the exercise of free choice in education and the democratization of educational opportunity. We can dispose of these points relatively quickly. The first problem is simply that affluent parents give their children tied money; youth are bribed to continue in school through the university years whereas they will receive no comparable parental subsidies if they leave school earlier to go to work. It may be argued that the "freedom to choose" must

be the parents' when it is not (as for the compulsory school years) the state's; but in that case we are in fact saying that parental hegemony should be extended on into adulthood, for the rich but not for the poor. This, of course, brings us to the matter of income distribution once again. Inequality is not just that some are poor. It is also that some are rich. And it is in part for this latter reason that no society has begun to develop efficient capital markets for the financing of education, as an investment in the acquisition both of future earning power and of potentials for greater enjoyments in the future.

(3) *Free tuition is antidemocratic*—and in a very direct and unambiguous way. The fortunate, born into homes in which they had early advantages of many kinds, are overrepresented in the universities of all countries. It is in the main to these relatively privileged young people that the general public is extending special grants for education, with special opportunities to earn more in the future and to prepare their children in turn to take advantage of educational opportunities. The perverse effects are most extreme where the less privileged have already been filtered during earlier grades of school that could qualify for university. But the effects are serious enough even in so open a system as that of the United States, where there is as wide a representation of the population in the universities as anywhere in the world. At the same time, the United States, followed by Japan, is the country in which the largest proportion of the direct cost of university education is covered by the students or their families. It is in countries with relatively small proportions attending universities that the students and their families are paying the smallest share of the costs. Nevertheless, recent studies suggest that the proportion of total education subsidies received by families in the higher-income group exceeds the proportions of taxes they pay over a large part of the United States. That free tuition, with or without subsistence allowances for all university students, is a democratically perverse measure in countries such as Sweden or the Netherlands—let alone in Latin America—seems virtually certain.

An alternative, obviously, is full tuition payment by those who can afford it, with scholarship assistance to those who cannot. Yes, I know what one of the replies to this will be: "That would be charity." Here I must confess that I do not see why receiving something "free" should be "charity" when the recipient needs it but not "charity" when he is rich. What sophistry is this that says gifts must be brought to the rich on behalf of the poor, to protect the latter from "charity." Is there something so disgraceful about being unable to pay one's way through college that it has to be concealed by such hypocrisy? The difficulties with the ability-to-pay criterion are surely of another order. Some would object to revealing information about personal income, but this is becoming less important and we may let it pass. Rarely mentioned, second, is the fact that this policy would reintroduce the problem of distortions in the signals for choice, discussed earlier, but among less affluent or poor people only. Perhaps that bias is desirable, however, since it would encourage choices in favor of more education among precisely those groups where we may especially want such a bias—as part of a broader long-term program for equalization of opportunity over the generations.

(4) *A meritocracy is antidemocratic, too.* I enjoy teaching and associating with intelligent people. I like to see them in the universities, and I am not willing to recommend that we do away with ability qualifications for entry; among other things, I should hate to dispose of incentives to intellectual achievement coordinate with ability. But let us be honest about it. That preference has nothing to do with being "democratic" or with "democratizing" the educational system. And selection by intelligence (if we could really identify it) has nothing to do with morals or equity. It is because relatively intelligent people (or those who pass as such) exercise the power and write the books and lay out the educational plans that they have been able to plant so firmly the notion that somehow individuals deserve more credit (or any credit) for being born with brains than being born with money.[28] People who do not have brains are at a disadvantage when it comes to talking back, that is obvious; more important, and more subtle, is the fact that they will normally accept an implicit (or even overt) disparagement of their quality as men, whatever the fine words about the equal value of every human being or being "born equal." Once we set aside arguments about efficiency and "external benefits," nothing is left of the notion that access to educational opportunity should (or could) be democratized by substituting selection by brains for selection by money. In fact the latter might be the less offensive to human dignity! Perhaps we should turn this all the way round. Those born with a big dose of human capital to start with have a head start over everyone else. If we extend the old idea of noblesse oblige, the brainy owe a special obligation to the rest of society who have been less fortunate in their genes.

The past decade has brought us into the era of mass elites. That era will work itself out through the decades immediately ahead, amid many contradictions and uncertainties. But there must be some wondering, right now, about those "others" who are not of the mass elites—the "others" who have often been forgotten in the absorption with what seemed to be the forefront of "democratic" change. Perhaps the new frontiers for the 1970's will be somewhere else; for there are little children, too.

Notes

1. Not all sorts of schooling, in all places, passed this test, of course. And there were plenty of disagreements. The important thing is that the times, the educators, and the (chosen) economists were "in harmony," on educational expansion, for a while at least.

2. See my essay on "The Costing of Human Resource Development" and discussions of that essay in E. A. G. Robinson and J. E. Vaizey (eds.), *The Economics of Education,* Proceedings of a Conference held by the International Economic Association (London: Macmillan, 1966), 421-50, 689-708.

3. There are many reasons why this tendency is most extreme in France. Interestingly enough, it finds a parallel among the ranks of economists. With a few notable exceptions, French economists can be divided roughly into two groups. There are the older literary economists, whose humanism is not usually challenged but whose expertise in modern economic theory and methodology is usually limited. And there are the new, modern French economists trained initially not in economics, but in engineering. French economists with a firm grounding in the foundations of modern economics and decision theory are highly exceptional.

4. W. D. Halls, "Educational Innovation in France," 1968 (mimeo), 78.

5. Somewhat to my initial surprise, I discovered recently that I can count as a "radical economist"—as radical as a long line of bearded (and not-so-bearded) men, from Adam Smith in 1776 through Karl Marx and Alfred Marshall and A. C. Pigou (which brings us past World War I)—and a good deal more radical than some men of 1970 who are busily preaching the rebellions of the 1920's.

6. Organization for Economic Cooperation and Development, *Development of Secondary Education* (Paris: O.E.C.D., 1969), 37.

7. *Ibid.,* 12.

8. *Ibid.,* 12, 14.

9. *Ibid.,* 96.

10. Organization for Economic Cooperation and Development, Directorate for Scientific Affairs, *Some Problems of the Development of Higher Education in Europe* (Paris: O.E.C.D., 1969), 27-28.

11. Edmund King, "Commentary on the Article by Professor Kazamias on Gentlemanly Culture in a Welfare State," for the conference on Cross-National

and Inter-Disciplinary Analysis of European Secondary Educational Reforms, held at Kent State University, Ohio, August 21-29, 1969 (mimeo), 5.

12. Seymour Harris, *The Market for College Graduates* (Cambridge, Mass.: Harvard University Press, 1959).

13. O.E.C.D., Directorate for Scientific Affairs, *op. cit.*, 36.

14. Or, in some cases, a notion of manpower "fit." However, manpower economists are taking a much more flexible view on this matter today than a few years ago.

15. Organization for Economic Cooperation and Development, *Statistics of the Occupational and Educational Structure of the Labour Force in 53 Countries* (Paris: O.E.C.D., 1969), 93.

16. The Central Council for Education, *Interim Report on Fundamental Policies and Measures for the Overall Expansion and Development of School Education in Future* (Tokyo: Ministry of Education, Japan, June 30, 1969), 44. Hereafter I shall designate this publication simply as Japan, *Interim Report.*

17. U.S. Census of Population, 1960.

18. At the Higher Education Research Unit, London School of Economics. For most European countries no estimates of any kind had been attempted before 1968-69, and in some there is still a data void.

19. O.E.C.D., *Development of Secondary Education,* 57, gives data for member countries on pass rates as a percent of entrants to senior secondary schools. The Japanese figures run from 94 to 96 percent whereas, in most of the other countries reporting, the proportions were in the range 40 to 60 percent. (Spanish upper secondary pupils matched the Japanese.)

20. *Ibid.*, p. 35.

21. An ingenious analysis is included in Richard Freeman, *The Markets for College Trained Manpower* (Cambridge, Mass.: Harvard University Press, 1971).

22. The Japanese Central Council for Education discusses this matter and makes explicit reference to the past history of progressive raising of compulsory education requirements. See Japan, *Interim Report,* 115ff.

23. *Ibid.*, 6.

24. *Ibid.*, 12.

25. *Ibid.*, 78.

26. *Ibid.*, 4.

27. *Ibid.*, 30.

28. In connection with these and related problems, see C. A. Anderson, "Dilemmas of Talent-Centered Educational Programs," *Year Book of Education 1962,* 445-57.

9. Equality versus Freedom

Hans A. Schieser

Is Quality Really Self-evident?

We hold these truths to be self-evident:
That all men are created equal . . .

Looking around, one finds everything but equality. People are different in age, sex, race, physical constitution, character, and less visible traits. None of them chose to be a woman or a man; nor did they decide which nationality or cultural background their parents should have. They were already "created" with differences, and, before becoming aware of them, the family and society shaped them in ways that cannot easily be reversed. Deep-rooted thought patterns formed in early childhood determine much of human behavior and result in additional differences. Even when an individual reaches maturity and becomes critical of his background, any attempt to alter or uproot the ideas or the experiences of the past is not easy. Adjustment to equalizing forces often results in emotional problems and other difficulties, as psychologists point out.

The founding fathers could not have pondered about "archetypes" and other roots of existential differences in man, but they must have seen the vast variety of human existence. The truth and "evidence" of their sentence on equality must, therefore, lie in another dimension.

Philosophy attempts an explanation by making the distinction between the "physical" and "metaphysical" dimensions of man. Jacques Maritain, for example, speaks of the *individual* as the observable, objective aspect of human existence, and the *person* as man's metaphysical essence which is independent of any physical appearance and functionality.[1]

The meaning of man's individuality is already indicated in the word itself: man is a "one," indivisible and unique in his physique. Throughout nature this is visible: even on the molecular level of matter "individual differences" within the same types can be discerned. For example, water molecules cluster in typical patterns at freezing temperatures, but each one of the ice crystals is different when one looks more closely. The same is true within the more complex structures of living organisms. Even so-called identical twins are far from being "identical" as individuals. On the other side, the metaphysical aspects of man, as they are independent of matter (*meta-physical,* meaning beyond matter), postulate a common denominator and values that cannot be discerned and measured.

The concept of human dignity may serve as an example here. If the tentative definition of *dignity* as *value* is acceptable, there can be meaning in the statement about man's equality. The value of man, as it is linked with his metaphysical essence, must remain independent of his individuality, that is, his health, intelligence, race, or functionality. In other words, regardless of an individual's usefulness to society, his personality must be respected and valued equally with that of a highly efficient citizen. Only then can we explain why society spends so much effort and money on the support of such burdensome and unproductive individuals as the retarded and the severely handicapped. At the same time, racial, sexual, and cultural discrimination become a denial of the dignity of man.

Many people reject the notion of a metaphysical reality. Can this be, when one speaks of a "self-evident truth"? An educator's experience with deviant "personalities" (or, more accurately, "individuals," if one accepts the above distinction) can make him skeptical concerning human dignity. Often, the brutality of human behavior conceals such dignity. It is not easy for a teacher to believe in the potential and value of a highly aggressive and violent pupil, and yet, to help such a child, such faith is necessary for evidence to the contrary may not emerge until a later stage of the child's development. In education one cannot wait for evidence of a child's worth and dignity; help must be based on the a priori assumption that the child is worth the effort.

The founding fathers must have had this equality in mind when they formulated the Declaration of Independence. They may, however, have used an a priori assumption of human dignity as the key to an understanding of the idea of a "United States of America" as a "Land of the Free," an idea that has been perverted by an emphasis on the physical dimension of equality and a denial of the a priori acceptance of a metaphysical equality of man.

The Idea of the "Land of the Free" and Its Perversion

The history of mankind suggests that the idea of equality is far from being "self-evident." In all societies there has been a clear tendency to label those who were different by race or creed or nationality as "strange" or "alien," and they were either forced to conform or they were expelled. The persecutions of particular groups going on in our century show that prejudice and intolerance against the "unequal" have not yet been overcome.

In 1780 the Swiss educator Pestalozzi urged political authorities and educators to solve the problems of poverty and injustice by providing for man's "most fundamental and natural need, which is equal for the rich and the poor: to have a *Heimat*," that is, a place where he is "at home," where he belongs and where he can enjoy peace.[2] Pestalozzi realized that man has his roots in the environment or "world" in which he matures and that continuous emotional ties to this home-world (*Heimat*) provide the basis of a fulfilled life:

The sphere of knowledge from which man in his individual station can receive happiness is limited; its sphere begins closely around him, around his own self and his nearest relationships, from there . . . it will expand, and while expanding it must regulate itself to this firm centre of all powers of truth . . .[3]

This insight, now confirmed by social psychology and experience with alienated and uprooted youth, was not well received in Europe at that time. Thousands lived in ghettos or were forced to leave their homelands to find a true *Heimat* in the New World. There it was possible, for the first time in man's history, to be accepted and welcomed with a guarantee that one could pursue happiness. In this land, there was to be no discussion about national, racial, or religious backgrounds before one was admitted. All were to be equally welcome and respected:

> Give me your tired, your poor,
> Your huddled masses,
> Yearning to breathe free,
> The wretched refuse of your teeming shore.
>
> Send these, the homeless,
> Tempest-tossed, to me;
> I lift up my lamp
> Beside the golden door![4]

The emphasis in the New World was not on equality but on freedom, and the role of the state was primarily to "guarantee the pursuit of happiness." No "Loyalty Oath" or "First Papers" were required for admission; nor was there any pressure to abandon traditions, languages, life styles, and faiths brought from the Old World. There was space for all. Up to this day we find the Mennonites, the Pennsylvania Dutch, and others with life styles retained through generations.

In contrast, the Puritans in New England attempted to use the New World to establish a new society for all—the same faith and the same life style. Cotton Mather angrily labeled Roger Williams "the first rebel against the Divine Church order established in the wilderness," which only marked the beginning of what would eventually distort the whole idea of America as the "Land of the Free," a *Heimat* for all who chose freedom over an imposed equality. What Pestalozzi saw in Europe—"the oppressive power of tyranny, privation of all enjoyment of truth, of happiness; unnatural absence of general national enlightenment concerning the fundamental interests and conditions of man . . ."[5] —appeared also in America. The fundamental interests of man became secondary to the interests of society, industry, and a national state.

The Declaration of Independence is based on the assumption that the pursuit of happiness is one of the most fundamental interests of man. There is no hint as to a particular happiness. Each citizen should pursue his own, and the authority of the state should guarantee this without unjust interference. In other words, all should be equally free in this pursuit, and only justice would require occasional regulation. Evolving communities were characterized by this pattern, and it seemed that they were following Pestalozzi's advice, wherein "man toils in his vocation and bears the burden of communal duties in order to enjoy his home in harmony and peace."[6] But Pestalozzi also warned that "to this peaceful enjoyment, man's education for his vocation and for his social ranks must be subordinated."[7]

Soon the scene was to change, however. With the development of a "national state," the emphasis on freedom and metaphysical foundations of equality shifted to a more literal understanding of equality. "America" was now to supersede the small worlds of the various immigrant groups, and happiness was more or less defined. Attempts were made to "Americanize" the newcomers and change their unique life styles in order to make everybody happy the "American way." An emerging industry required more man power, and this demand created problems of social justice and prompted the search for an "equalizer and balancing wheel" that would be effective in diverse society. Education was seen as being the best vehicle for achieving this standardization.

This assumption did not prove valid. Providing equal access to schools did not result in more equality; nor did it do away with prejudice and social injustice. Some people still wonder whether a Catholic can be a good American; others cannot understand why an alien resident chooses not to become a citizen even though he might have been living in the United States for many years. The misconception of equality has led to strange outgrowths of pedantry, and the recent trend to "balance" employment figures in terms of race and sex, regardless of competencies and human qualities, is a questionable and sometimes ridiculous way to establish "equal opportunity."

It is necessary to rethink the concept of equality. Rethinking must not be confused with reacting, however.

Reacting against the Perversion of Equality and Rethinking the Ideal of Equality

The young generation is highly critical of the "myth" of America as it has been described to them, a disillusionment not confined to the New World alone. In all nations with a developed *National-bewusstsein* (national feeling or awareness or identity), the validity of national ideals has been scrutinized, even denied. The attitude of some of the athletes from the United States during the Olympic Games in Munich was a symptom of the rejection of the symbolic nation. The emergence of a so-called youth culture may well be reaction against an imposed abstract concept that does not exist in the concrete experience of man. What one knows and loves is not the "nation" but the concrete reality of his immediate environment, his *Heimat*. This may be a residential area in a big city or a remote ranch in the mountains, but it is never an abstract "country" with political boundaries, symbolic emblems, and a national government. The attempt to superimpose feelings of patriotism and love for the nation has all too often been misused to achieve cohesiveness and equality under one flag to promote national interests, most often at the expense of the subjects. When youth turns to the concrete reality of community, nature, and the like, their preoccupations may be problematic at times, but they are a reaction against the hollow ideals which they never saw realized. In other words, young people do not want to be equal; they want to do "their own thing" and be different. The tragedy is that, in the attempt, they sometimes conform even more, but at least their concern for the authentic should be acknowledged. The romanticism of those who flee the cities for the "life in the woods" cannot be cured with slogans which we do not even believe ourselves. A serious rethinking of what America stands for and what is really meant by equality, freedom, and dignity is needed, not an angry backlash.

The first question to be considered in such a rethinking would be whether or not one accepts a priori human dignity and the fundamental rights that are connected with it. If so, then one cannot envisage any form of equality that would run counter to man's freedom to pursue happiness.

Any attempt by a government or other authorities in society to declare and enforce "what is good for all" on any sector of life becomes questionable in light of pursuing happiness through freedom. The concrete case of public education may serve as a paradigm here. While we adhere to the inalienable right of parents to determine the education of their children, at the same time we force some parents to send their children to schools which they do not like. Constitutionalists who insist on the "separation of church and state" in the case of subsidies to private schools give priority to a secondary principle meant to prevent a questionable equality, but they betray a primary and fundamental principle that is the very basis of a free democracy, the principle of subsidiarity. This principle says that the authority of the state is founded on the right of any citizen to find help when he needs it and when he himself or his nearest social circles cannot help in important matters. When education is conceived as an important matter, and when parents are forced by circumstances to expose their children to undesired influences—they need not necessarily be harmful—then they have a right to find help. Otherwise, parents are not free to determine the education of their children. On the other side, one must admit that the public schools, once conceived as a vehicle for equalization of opportunity, have now become the receptacle for those children whose parents cannot afford a better school. This is true in many metropolitan areas. How it can be reconciled with equality and justice is a question which should occupy defenders of the Constitution much more than the casuistry which is in vogue.

If the original conception of man in our culture is no longer valid and if other categories than those used by the founding fathers must be found, a completely different concept of equality could emerge. Whoever assumes the authority to define happiness for others and claims infallibility in matters pertaining to the "common good" will face opposition. Religion provides a classic example of an attempt to force equality for the sake of salvation. Even saints occasionally suffered from such well-meant but questionable practices.

The state, however, has far surpassed what any Inquisition ever did to heretics. The concentration camps and witch hunts of this century (not all in other countries!) have all been justified by those who "know what is good for the people!" There is undoubtedly "equality" when dissenters and nonconformists are expelled or "liquidated," but where is freedom and respect for human dignity?

No government can nowadays "run" a country alone without becoming a totalitarian system. In a free country, all agencies of society—churches, economic and political structures, interest groups of all sorts—cooperate to ensure the pursuit of happiness. Any complete separation of the state from such agencies is impossible. The withdrawal of all privately run schools would prove disastrous, as would the closing of church-owned hospitals and other institutions. Most modern states have realistically considered this even though they avoid religious affiliation, economic regulation, and other connections. America now faces a trend that runs counter to officially declared neutrality in such matters. The government takes over tasks which originally have been in the hands of other institutions of society, and it helps where no help is needed. The resulting standardization has many advantages, but there is also an equalization that dangerously resembles the practices of an "almighty state" in a totalitarian setting. The development of a welfare state to achieve equal medical help and support for the aged, for example, has created more inequality and injustice, not to speak of infringement on individual freedom. It would be sufficient, and more consistent with the principle of subsidiarity, if the government would exercise reliable controls over such services so that a minimum of quality and reliability is guaranteed, instead of developing a monolithic system with no alternatives. While these examples may represent extreme cases, they nevertheless demonstrate that a concept of equality is based on the denial of human rights. The complexity of contemporary life cannot be met with practices of the eighteenth century, but respect for man's dignity remains as a basis for legislation, economic and political.

Equality, Freedom, and Human Dignity

I cannot accept Skinner's contention that we are "beyond freedom and dignity" unless we advocate the totalitarianism of a system that controls not only behavior but also man's whole existence. The attempt to generate a homogeneous, equal generation of "good citizens" in test tubes and by a close-knit system of education through behavior modification would most likely lead to a "new world" of total equality. There might be hope that this will never happen as the unpredictability of the human mind (and that of rats, as Skinner may have found out) ensures that there is a fallout of some individuals where technology does not work. But the fact that techniques of equalization do work with the masses should make us aware of imminent dangers. The examples of a Hitler and other dictators of our time challenge us to rethink our ideals not only historically, but also with a view toward implications for the future.

Equality in education may have been a genuine concern at a time when education was the privilege of a leisure class; it could result in a monolithic system of public schooling with a monopoly in indoctrination. In this respect, the inequalities of a pluralistic system provide the best safeguard for freedom.

It seems that the concept of equality cannot be separated from the ideal of freedom. Both constitute a polarity between which human existence takes place: the more freedom we allow, the less visible equality we may expect. Societies that emphasize equality in concrete matters cannot avoid limiting the freedom of the people. The only "beyond" we can allow here is the metaphysical dimension of man's existence: that dignity which entitles all equally to those rights to which we subscribe in our democracy.

Notes

1. See Jacques Maritain, *The Person and the Common Good* (South Bend, Ind.: Notre Dame University Press, 1966).

2. See Johann Heinrich Pestalozzi, *Evening Hour of a Hermit* (1780), excerpts translated in R. Ulich, *Three Thousand Years of Educational Wisdom* (Cambridge, Mass.: Harvard University Press, 1965), 481-85.

3. *Ibid.*, 481-82.

4. Inscription on the Statue of Liberty, New York Harbor.

5. Pestalozzi, *Evening Hour*, 483.

6. *Ibid*, 484.

7. *Ibid.*

10. The Public School: Assaults on a Great Idea

R. Freeman Butts

Of all the unsettling results of the malaise of the 1960's the most ominous may be the erosion of America's faith in public education as a cultural and social element in building a sense of national community. This weakening of commitment to public education stems partly from a resurgence of older separatist and centrifugal tendencies in American society, and partly from the thrashing about for ways to loosen up what is described as a rigid and inhumane system. It reflects a general loss of respect for authority in government, school, university, church, and community arising from the war in Vietnam, the youth counterculture, demands for cultural separatism, and the militant search for racial or ethnic identity.

The general quest for "alternatives" to the existing system is in part deliberately designed to weaken public education, in part unaware that it may have that effect. It is the convergence and mutual reinforcement of so many forces—political, social, economic, racial, religious, and intellectual—that makes the search for "alternatives" so beguiling. But if the American people should become disenchanted with the idea of the public school and turn in significant numbers to

Reprinted with permission from *The Nation* (April 30, 1973), 16-24.

other means of education, they will weaken, perhaps beyond repair, a basic component of democratic American society.

The clamor for "alternatives" undermines the basic meaning of the public school, which was hammered out in the considerable consensus achieved during nearly two centuries of American history. That there was a consensus may be seen in the fact that by 1900 about 92 percent of elementary and secondary school children were in public schools. Thereafter, major efforts by religious groups doubled the proportion of children in nonpublic schools by the 1960's (to 14 or 15 percent), but this enrollment has since declined to around 10 percent. The fact that 90 percent of American children are today in public schools does not necessarily mean that all the aspects of public education discussed below are universally accepted, but they are identifiable elements of the public school idea. In the consensus, public schools have been characterized primarily as having a public purpose, public control, public support, public access, and public commitment to civic unity.

A public school serves a public purpose rather than a private one. It is not maintained for the personal advantage or private gain of the teacher, the proprietor, or the board of managers; nor does it exist simply for the enjoyment, happiness, or advancement of the individual student or his parents. It may, indeed it should, enhance the vocational competence, or upward social mobility, or personal development of individuals, but if that were all a school attempted, the job could be done as well by a private school catering to particular jobs, or careers or leisure-time enjoyment.

 Rather, the prime purpose of the public school is to serve the general welfare of a democratic society, by assuring that the knowledge and understanding necessary to exercise the responsibilities of citizenship are not only made available but actively inculcated. "If," said Thomas Jefferson, "a nation expects to be ignorant and free, in a state of civilization, it expects what never was and never will be."

Achieving a sense of community is the essential purpose of public education. This work cannot be left to the vagaries of individual parents, or small groups of like-minded parents, or particular interest groups, or religious sects, or private enterprisers or cultural specialties. Thus, when the population became ever more heterogeneous after the mid-nineteenth century, the need for compulsory education became increasingly apparent to the lawmakers of the states and of the Union.

Today, however, this basic point is almost entirely overlooked in the furor over the studies of inequality in schools, stemming from the Coleman report of 1966 and expanded upon since by the studies at Harvard of Daniel Patrick Moynihan, Christopher Jencks, and others. Their generalizations that public schools have not overcome economic inequality among races or social classes have led to a general impression that public schools do not make much difference and that the compensatory education advocated by reformers since the mid-1960's has generally failed. Economy-minded politicians pick up this theme with glee, and racial minorities are discouraged that, just as they are finally making some headway toward equal opportunity in the schools, the word comes down from the scholars, "Don't bother; the public schools don't really matter that much."

To make matters worse, Ivan Illich, Everett Reimer and other radical critics preach that the schools are really instruments of oppression whereby the ruling class maintains itself in power and instills in the other classes attitudes of subservience designed to support the status quo. Illich and Reimer argue that, to effect genuine social change, the society must be "deschooled" and all kinds of informal and nonformal means of community education fostered instead. Compulsory attendance must be abolished, so that children, youth, and adults of the oppressed classes may be free to develop their distinctive talents and not be forced into a mold by a monolithic and oppressive public school system.

So the discussion has focused on the *economic* inequalities among classes and races and the inability of public schools to remedy what the entire society has wrought. However, there is still enormous disagreement about these generalizations. The historic and comparative evidence is overwhelming that American public schools have been one major factor in producing a higher per capita economic level in America than in any other country, but that is not the critical point here. Even if Jencks should turn out to be right, that compensatory education for the disadvantaged in our society is unable to reduce the economic gap between the rich and the poor, the *economic* argument is not and never has been the fundamental reason for compensatory education. That reason is the public purpose of *justice*. Our conception of a just society based upon principles of liberty and equality requires a public education available to all.

John Rawls, professor of philosophy at Harvard, sees this point more clearly than do his colleagues in the social sciences and education. In order to provide genuine equality of opportunity a just society must give special attention to those born into less favorable social positions. "The value of education should not be assessed only in terms of economic efficiency and social welfare. Equally if not more important is the role of education in enabling a person to enjoy the culture of his society and *to take part in its affairs,* and in this way to provide for each individual a *secure sense of his own worth*" (*A Theory of Justice* [Cambridge, Mass.: Harvard University Press]).

If public schools also enable the disadvantaged to improve their economic position, as I believe in the long run they undoubtedly do, that is a social dividend, but the original purpose of public education in the early nineteenth century was not to provide vocational education or prepare people for jobs. That addendum came along in response to the industrialization and technological specialization of the economy in the later nineteenth and early twentieth centuries. To make the achievement of equal economic condition appear to be the *prime* purpose of public schools and to dismiss rather casually the school system as a "marginal institution" because it does not produce the equality (as Jencks does) is to ignore the fundamental *political* purpose of public education. In the words of Justice Frankfurter, "The school should be the training ground for habits of community." *That* is the ground on which the public schools should be criticized for failure, and where effort should be exerted for improvement. And that is the area in which there really is no genuine alternative to the public schools.

A public school is one that is under the control of public authorities who own and manage the schools and who are responsible to the people either directly by election or indirectly through publicly designated officers of the civil government. It is significant that Americans speak of "public" schools rather than of "state" or "government" schools, as is the custom in many countries. The term signifies an institution that is directly responsible to the people rather than to one of the legislative, executive, or judicial branches of government. Indeed, the distinctive form of school government (the elected lay board of education) was intended to keep the public school responsive to local community interests, yet somewhat free of the narrow partisan politics or bureaucratic controls of the other branches of local government.

In the nineteenth century it was hoped that a balance would be struck between a central and common authority lodged in the state constitutions, state legislatures, and state departments of education, and a flexible operation and management lodged in the local boards of education. However, in the twentieth century the matter of control became more complicated when the federal courts increasingly acknowledged their responsibility to interpret the principles of freedom and equality as defined in the Bill of Rights and applied them to all public schools in the states. Although Americans habitually say that public education is a state and not a federal matter, the most difficult and sensitive problems in the past two decades have arisen over federal constitutional issues in the areas of religion and racial segregation.

And in this process the public schools have become a battleground for control by special group interests, some feeling justified because they believe they have not had a fair share in the control of "their" public schools, and others because they have feared the intrusion of "outsiders" into "their" neighborhood schools. The demand of blacks in the urban centers for "community control" or for decentralization is one example of the asserted need to shape local schools to the desires of local groups rather than that such groups be forced to accept teachers or budgets or curricula handed down from some unsympathetic and remote bureaucracy. On the other hand, local white "communities" have declared the right to keep their neighborhood schools white, on the principle of local control and in defiance of desegregation orders by federal courts or central educational authorities.

But the struggles over control are complicated far beyond the question of desegregation. A resurgence of hostility to bureaucratic formalism has led to demands for greater free enterprise in the domain of education. This discontent ranges from demands for "free" or "open" schools to outcries against curriculum or professional requirements that particular groups have felt were irrelevant to their special interests. This attitude fits with the clamor for parents' "freedom of choice" to determine the kind of education they want for their children—whether segregated education for white or blacks only, or religious education for Catholics or Protestants or Jews only, or political education for radicals or conservatives only. And as the clamor has grown it has seemed easy to argue that such goals could be better achieved by "alternative" schools. So a southern reaction to desegregation orders was to seek ways to abolish the free public schools and set up free private schools (with public funds, of course). Some advocates of private enterprise saw this as an opening to get public support for proprietary schools of many kinds. Others saw it as an opportunity to claim that private companies could do a better educational job in the public schools than could the teaching profession, and "performance contracts" were signed with some boards of education to deliver the educational goods for a price and with an efficiency that would outmode the traditional faculty. So far, the evidence in favor of "performance contracting" is dubious, to say the least.

Demands for "accountability" and "management efficiency" and "competency-based teacher education" added heat to the arguments over who should control what in the public schools. Meanwhile, the organized teaching profession has launched collective bargaining struggles in most major cities over matters of salary, appointment, tenure, and benefits. This has brought teachers and administrators into confrontation not only with the elected boards of education but also with "community demands" that teachers be black or white or religious or ethnic in conformity with the majorities in given neighborhoods. There is no doubt that militancy improves the conditions of professional employment, but it also raises uneasy questions about the control of public schools.

In many of the struggles for control the interests of special groups have taken precedence over the search for rational allocations of authority among local, state, and national requirements. The *constitutional* commands of the First Amendment for liberty and the Fourteenth Amendment for equality are in danger of being lost in the uproar, as they have been lost in other aspects of the political process.

The tendency has been to assume that the public school systems are bureaucratically rigid and must be bent to serve the interests of disparate groups. And if the public schools are harmed in the process, too bad; they were not all that good anyway. The need, rather, is to devise ways of reconciling diverse individual and group freedoms with the common and general freedom. Somehow, as Rawls puts it, in a just society each person is to have an equal right to the most extensive total system of equal basic liberties compatible with a similar system of liberty for all; and any social or economic inequalities are to be so arranged that they adhere to the greatest benefit of the least advantaged. Control of the public schools should be sought in these terms, not simply as means to serve majority or minority or group interests locked in combat.

A public school is primarily supported by public funds raised by taxation at the local, state, and federal levels. It does not rely heavily on direct financial charges upon the student or his parents in the form of fees or tuition. Support of education through general taxation was achieved only after a long and bitter fight. It had to overcome the belief that education depended on parental ability to pay and that private tuition was a perfectly natural way to obtain education along with other social goods. But the appeal to the public good gradually won a consensus that general taxation was the only means by which education could be made available to all comers no matter what their economic status.

From the beginning, however, it was clear that local school districts would differ widely in their ability to support public schools or indeed in their willingness to tax themselves for the purpose. The states have thus gone through long and complicated procedures to require local districts to tax themselves and to try to equalize the provision of schooling by all sorts of financial formulas for state aid. In recent years it is even being argued (in the *Serrano* case in California) that the local property tax system is essentially so unequal in its ability to provide educational facilities that it violates the Fourteenth Amendment's command for equal protection of the laws; states may thus have to turn from local property taxes for the purpose and adopt statewide taxation.

While the U.S. Supreme Court, by [a vote of] 5 to 4, denied this line of argument in a Texas case during March, the New Jersey Supreme Court ruled in April that the New Jersey constitutional requirement for equal educational opportunity outlaws the local property tax as the prime means of support for public schools. Furthermore, the rapidly increased use of federal funds represented by the Elementary and Secondary School Act of 1965 recognized, at least implicitly, that inequality of resources among the states would necessitate a federal basis for public school support.

But just when it began to look as though federal support of public schools would finally begin to make a difference, some 200 years after the first federal land grants were made under the ordinances of the 1780's, the clamor for public support of private and religious schools was renewed, this time aided by the President himself. During the nineteenth and most of the twentieth centuries Catholic opposition to federal aid (unless it included Catholic schools in the aid) had prevented the allocation of general federal funds for public schools. Finally, a compromise was reached in 1965 after a quiescent period of ecumenism in the early 1960's, and thereafter the drive for public funds for private schools gained momentum as the costs of schooling rose and enrollments in private schools dropped.

Whereas in the 1940's and 1950's the claims for public aid for parochial schools had been for auxiliary services such as bus transportation, textbooks, health services, and the like, now the campaign is for direct support, and gains have been made in many states for one form or another of public assistance: aid to private schools for buildings or for reimbursement of the costs of testing and record keeping required by the state (a New York State law of 1970 was struck down by a federal court in 1972); payment of salaries for teaching secular subjects (Pennsylvania and Rhode Island laws were struck down by the Supreme Court in June 1971); grants for tuition to low-income parents (Pennsylvania and New York laws were struck down by federal courts in 1972); and tax credits or rebates on income tax payments. Several of these cases are now before the Supreme Court, and a landmark decision is expected by June. Just a few weeks ago a federal court stopped payment of New Jersey state funds to private and parochial schools.

Again, these matters hinge upon the constitutional ban on the allocation of state funds to religious schools. But religious and other private groups have persistently argued that parents and churches have prior rights over the state in the realm of education. They insist that the public pool of tax moneys raised for public education should be divided among parents and churches to support schools of their choice.

And now comes along a plan whereby parents are given vouchers representing public funds, with which they can shop around among various "alternatives." Even the federal government through the Office of Economic Opportunity has promoted a trial of such schemes. In some cases the vouchers are good only within the public school system, but the principle can easily be extended by Roman Catholics to include their schools, or by private entrepreneurs to include theirs, or by white or black separatists to include theirs. A wholesale application of the idea would further undermine the public schools, whose budgets in recent years have encountered ever tougher resistance in local elections.

It is odd that President Nixon and Governor Rockefeller can plead on one hand the shortage of funds for public schools and at the same time promise Catholic voters that they will do all they can to assign tax funds to nonpublic schools. And revenue sharing will increase pressure at the local level to use the federal funds thus shared for nonpublic schools. Since social science investigators now claim that more money does not really improve the quality of education, it is curious that private schools still seem to think that more money would improve the quality of *their* schools. And still more curious is the outrage expressed against bussing to achieve desegregation in the public schools, when it is juxtaposed with the enthusiastic campaign to use public funds to *assist* bussing of children to parochial schools. In any case, the support of public schools from public funds is weakened whenever dissident groups press for their solutions rather than a public school solution.

Public schools are intended to provide access freely and openly to all persons, irrespective of class, religion, race, ethnic or national origin, or sex. Ideally, a public school is thus a school common to all in the society and does not discriminate among pupils on grounds other than educational achievement and age. As everyone knows, however, it was not until 1954 that the principle of equal access was defined unequivocally by the Supreme Court. Before that, the United States had long condoned a dual system of schools for blacks and whites, de jure in the South and de facto in many parts of the North and West; and with somewhat analogous conditions for American Indians on reservations, and for Spanish-speakers in the Southwest. But in the *Brown* decision the Supreme Court said, "We conclude that in the field of public education the doctrine of 'separate but equal' has no place. Separate educational facilities are inherently unequal." After nearly 150 years the racially disjunctive system of schools in the South began painfully and slowly to coalesce.

Then, as desegregation finally began to be accepted in the South after a decade of confrontations between state and federal authorities and violence in the schools and universities, the action shifted from the legal segregation in the South to the de facto segregation in the cities and suburbs of the North. And so the bussing issue came to the fore, as the courts agreed that, when all else failed, bussing had to be tried. Somehow, the Supreme Court said in April 1971, the dual school system had to be dismantled in conformity with the requirement of "equal protection of the laws" of the Fourteenth Amendment. Yet, while the proportion of blacks in majority white schools of the South had grown to some 40 percent, it remained at around 27 percent in the North and West, and in the large northern cities it was actually decreasing.

So not only did bussing become an explosive political issue by 1972 but also black nationalists themselves began to argue for separatism and seemed to retreat to resegregation in order to gain more control over their own community schools. In September 1970 the Congress of Racial Equality apparently rejected the goal of integration and officially adopted a public school plan in Mobile that would produce "desegregation without integration," a view scarcely distinguishable from the *Plessy* doctrine of "separate but equal."

At that point, the President and most political leaders were not only not trying to save the public school idea of open access in the face of the bussing clamor but were actually casting a fog over the once widely held faith in the value of common schools to be used by all segments of the community. This could be taken only as an official blessing to the white flight to the suburbs that had accelerated during the decade when the federal courts were defining the goals of integration and of equality demanded by the Constitution. Only a few voices were arguing that integrated public schools could be a powerful antidote for the racist attitudes that infected the country, North and South, East and West.

Too little thought was being given to the findings that black pupils did better in integrated schools, or that, even if they did not do better academically, they were spared the damage to personality and self-respect endemic in the dual system. It had become clear to the peoples of the world that the most virulent residue of the colonial empires was the resentment against the psychological degradation of being treated as inferiors by colonial masters. What white Americans could not seem to understand was that a similar resentment among blacks was a bitter residue of the dual school system and of continuing humiliation in schools where legal desegregation had been achieved but genuine integration had not even been tried. What was forgotten was that a major task of a public school system was to achieve a truly integrative social and cultural atmosphere wherein students could learn the meaning of mutual dignity, acceptance, and self-respect across social and ethnic lines. But that is a task which the public schools cannot adequately undertake while beset by drives to resegregation or separatism, whether in the city ghettos or in the suburban gardens. And if the Nixon Supreme Court should reverse or substantially weaken the constitutional decisions of two decades, the cause would become immeasurably more difficult.

Finally, public schools have a commitment to elevate the civic goal of unity above the particularist goals of special and self-serving interests in the society. This is one of the most sensitive and complicated of all the tasks of public education, for it is extremely difficult to draw the line between the values of diversity (which a democratic society prizes) and of divisiveness (which may threaten the very society itself). Most modern school systems in the world are torn by two conflicting drives: on the one hand, to help build national unity out of diverse racial, cultural, ethnic, religious, and linguistic groups, and, on the other, to honor the drive of particularist groups that demand their own schools for the teaching of different languages, religious beliefs, ethnic customs, or regional aspirations. The modernizing world abounds in examples. In 1947 India and Pakistan had to divide along such lines before each could start to build a nation. Since then, India has struggled with the surging forces of more than a dozen major languages, while irreconcilable Bangladesh has split off from Pakistan. Nigeria averted a spin-off of a major ethnic group in its civil war. And a score of nations keep searching for ways to reconcile the separatist drives with the nation-building drive. Division among groups leads to demand for separate schools; separate schools in turn strengthen and perpetuate the group divisions.

The United States evaded the worst of the divisive cultural conflicts in the eighteenth and nineteenth centuries, mainly by forbidding the state to intrude in religious matters except to guarantee religious freedom for all. This separation of church and state did not come about easily; but with the adoption of the First Amendment in 1791 and with similar enactments in state constitutions, the worst of the religious violence and antagonisms that wracked Germany, France, the Netherlands, Italy, and Spain in the Reformation wars (and Northern Ireland to this day) were avoided here. To be sure, not all this has been sweetness and light, but in general the trend has been to reduce the religious and especially the sectarian characteristics of public schools over a period of 150 years. Sometimes this has been done on a principle of religious freedom and separation of church and state; sometimes on a purely pragmatic basis that diverse religious groups could not agree on the specifics of religious instruction, or doctrine, or creed, or devotional exercises that should be required of all children in a common school.

No matter what the reason, the ideal of the public school as a "symbol of our secular society" was nowhere better stated than by Mr. Justice Frankfurter in the *McCollum* case in 1948:

Designed to serve as perhaps the most powerful agency for promoting cohesion among a heterogeneous democratic people, the public school must keep scrupulously free from entanglement in the strife of sects. . . . The public school is at once the symbol of our democracy and the most pervasive means for promoting our common destiny. In no activity of the State is it more vital to keep out divisive forces than in its schools, to avoid confusing, not to say fusing, what the Constitution sought to keep strictly apart. "The great American principle of eternal separation"—Elihu Root's phrase bears repetition—is one of the vital reliances of our Constitutional system for assuring unities among our people stronger than our diversities. It is the Court's duty to enforce this principle in its full integrity.

But a short twenty-five years after this ringing declaration of faith in the public school, what do we find? Public education is being described by some of our radical revisionist historians of education as no more than illusion or legend or myth. Such radical critics know exactly what they are doing. They see the public school system as standing in the way of revolutionary social change, as do the other institutions of representative government, economy, and religion. But their arguments are only part of the story and probably not the most important part. The undermining of the idea of public education by conservatives, liberals, and the politically neutral or naïve is probably even more significant. For now, all five aspects of the meaning of public schools are being eroded in both direct and subtle ways, and when the entire picture is put together it is probably not too extreme to say that a basic reversal of one of our fundamental institutions may be looming for the first time in nearly two hundred years. Wouldn't it be ironically tragic if in 1976 we were to "celebrate" the bicentennial anniversary of the American Revolution by abolishing the public schools?

Lest this should happen, I believe that there must be a mobilization to insist that the public schools concentrate as they never have before on the task of building a sense of civic cohesion among all the people of the country. This should become the chief priority for educational planning, curriculum development, organization, research, and experimentation. I am not calling for a new patriotism of law and order, nor for loyalty oaths, nor a nationally imposed curriculum in "civics," nor flag salutes, nor recitation of prayers or pledges of allegiance. But I do believe that we require the renewal of a civic commitment that seeks to reverse and overcome the trend to segmented and disjunctive "alternatives" serving narrow or parochial or racist interests.

Our people are badly divided and dispirited, if not demoralized, by trials they underwent in the late 1960's and early 1970's. They badly need a spark to rekindle the sense of community. That is what the French meant when they coined the term *civisme* to denote the principles of good citizenship, the attitudes, virtues, and disposition devoted to the cause of the French Revolution of 1789. It was from a similar urgency that the founders of this country argued that a new republic needed an appropriately republican education to assure the stability and success of a democratic government and democratic society. The nation and the world are drastically different nearly two hundred years later, but that is only the more reason to concentrate on what the new civism should be and what the public education system should do.

I believe the chief end of American public education is the promotion of a new civism appropriate to the principles of a just society in the United States and a just world community. We have forgotten or simply mouthed these goals; now we must advance them in full seriousness as the first order of business for the future.

Whatever else the general guidelines of the new civism should be, they will be found by renewing the principles of justice, liberty, and equality summarized in the Bill of Rights of the Constitution and applied to the states by the Fourteenth Amendment. So far, the federal courts have seen this fact more clearly than have the legislatures or the politicians or the organized teaching profession itself. They have been more faithful to the basic meaning of public education than have the profession, the critics, the reformers, or the local or state boards of education.

We must take the judicial doctrines seriously. While the social scientists argue and wrangle over their empirical data, the people of America must preserve their public school system by concerted political action so that there will be something to improve. We can no more dismantle our public schools, or let them be eroded, than we can dismantle our representative government, or our courts or our free press. This is not to say that important changes are not necessary; it is to say that undermining free public education is tantamount to undermining the free society itself. In this respect the radicals are correct; the question is whether the government and the society are worth saving. It is my opinion that they are. Therefore I believe that public education must be rejuvenated.

It is a task worth the best efforts of all concerned citizens—professional organizations, political parties, voluntary groups, Common Cause, and all other good-government organizations. If we mean to maintain and improve a cohesive and just society based upon liberty, equality, and fraternal civism, there is no alternative to the public schools.

Selected Bibliography

Andrew T. Kopan and *Don T. Martin*

Books

Alloway, David N., and Francesco Cordasco. *Minorities and the American City: A Sociological Primer for Educators.* New York: David McKay Company, Inc., 1970.

Berg, Ivar E. *Education and Jobs: The Great Training Robbery.* Boston: Beacon Press, 1971.

Birley, Derek, and Anne Dufton. *An Equal Chance: Equalities and Inequalities of Educational Opportunity.* New York: Fernhill House, 1971.

Brickman, William W., and Stanley Lehrer. *Education and the Many Faces of the Disadvantaged: Cultural and Historical Perspectives.* New York: John Wiley and Company, 1972.

Carnoy, Martin, ed. *Schooling in a Corporate Society: The Political Economy of Education in America.* New York: David McKay Company, Inc., 1972.

Charnofsky, Stanley. *Educating the Powerless.* Belmont, Calif.: Wadsworth Publishing Company, Inc., 1971.

Coleman, James S., *et al. Equality of Educational Opportunity.* Washington, D.C.: U. S. Government Printing Office, 1966.

Conant, James B. *Slums and Suburbs.* New York: McGraw-Hill, 1961.

Duncan, Otis Dudley, David L. Featherware, and Beverly Duncan. *Socioeconomic Background and Achievement.* New York: Seminar Press, 1972.

Fantini, Mario D., Marilyn Gittell, and Richard Magat. *Community Control and the Urban School.* New York: Praeger Publishers, 1970.

Foster, Marcus A. *Making Schools Work: Strategies for Changing Education.* Philadelphia: Westminster Press, 1971.

Franklin, Raymond, and Solomon Resnik. *The Political Economy of Racism.* New York: Holt, Rinehart and Winston, 1973.

Freire, Paulo. *Pedagogy of the Oppressed.* New York: Herder and Herder, 1970.

Frost, Joe L., and Glenn R. Hawkes, eds. *The Disadvantaged Child: Issues and Innovations,* 2nd ed. Boston: Houghton Mifflin Company, 1970.

Ginsburg, Herbert. *The Myth of the Deprived Child: Poor Children's Intellect and Education.* Englewood Cliffs, N.J.: Prentice-Hall, 1972.

Gordon, David M., comp. *Problems in Political Economy: An Urban Perspective.* Lexington, Mass.: D. C. Heath, 1971.

Greer, Colin. *The Great School Legend: A Revisionist Interpretation of American Public Education.* New York: Basic Books, 1972.

Grier, William H., and Price M. Cobbs. *Black Rage.* New York: Basic Books, 1968.

Guthrie, James W., *et al. Schools and Inequality.* Cambridge: Massachusetts Institute of Technology Press, 1971.

Handlin, Oscar. *Race and Nationality in American Life.* Boston: Little, Brown & Company, 1957.

Harrison, Bennett. *Education, Training, and the Urban Ghetto.* Baltimore: Johns Hopkins University Press, 1972.

Haubrich, Vernon F., ed. *Freedom, Bureaucracy, and Schooling.* Washington, D.C.: Association for Supervision and Curriculum Development, NEA, 1971.

Havighurst, Robert J., ed. *Metropolitanism: Its Challenges to Education.* Sixty-seventh Yearbook of the National Society for the Study of Education, Part I. Chicago: University of Chicago Press, 1968.

Heath, G. Louis. *Red, Brown, and Black Demands for Better Education.* Philadelphia: Westminster Press, 1972.

Henderson, George, ed. *America's Other Children: Public Schools outside Suburbia.* Norman: University of Oklahoma Press, 1971.

Hillson, Maurie, Francesco Cordasco, and Francis P. Purcell, comps. *Education and the Urban Community: Schools and the Crisis of the Cities.* New York: American Book Company, 1969.

Illich, Ivan. *Deschooling Society.* New York: Harper and Row, 1971.

Itzkoff, Seymour W. *Cultural Pluralism and American Education.* Scranton, Pa.: International Textbook Company, 1969.

Jencks, Christopher, *et al. Inequality: A Reassessment of the Effect of Family and Schooling in America.* New York: Basic Books, 1972.

Karier, Clarence J., Paul Violas, and Joel Spring. *Roots of Crisis: American Education in the Twentieth Century.* Chicago: Rand-McNally and Company, 1973.

Katz, Michael B. *Class, Bureaucracy and Schools: The Illusion of Educational Change in America.* New York: Praeger Publishers, 1971.

Katzman, Martin. *The Political Economy of Urban Schools.* Cambridge, Mass.: Harvard University Press, 1971.

Kolko, Gabriel. *Wealth and Power in America.* New York: Praeger Publishers, 1962.

Kozol, Jonathan. *Death at an Early Age.* Boston: Houghton Mifflin Company, 1968.

Levine, Daniel, and Robert J. Havighurst, eds. *Farewell to Schools???* Worthington, Ohio: Charles A. Jones Publishing Company, 1971.

Longstreet, Wilma S. *Beyond Jencks: The Myth of Equal Schooling.* Washington, D.C.: Association for Supervision and Curriculum Development, NEA, 1973.

Miller, Gordon W. *Educational Opportunity and the Home.* New York: Humanities Press, 1971.

Miller, Harry L., ed. *Education for the Disadvantaged.* New York: The Free Press, 1967.

Mosteller, Frederick, and Daniel P. Moynihan. *On Equality of Educational Opportunity.* New York: Random House, 1972.

Passow, A. Harry, ed. *Urban Education in the 1970s.* New York: Teachers College Press, 1971.

Pringle, M. L. Kellner. *Deprivation and Education,* 2nd ed. New York: Humanities Press, 1971.

Rawls, John. *A Theory of Justice.* Cambridge, Mass.: Belknap Press of Harvard University Press, 1971.

Riessman, Frank. *The Culturally Deprived Child.* New York: Harper and Row, 1962.

Roberts, Joan I., ed. *School Children in the Urban Slum.* New York: The Free Press, 1967.

Rubin, Lillian B. *Busing and Backlash.* Berkeley: University of California Press, 1972.

Sackrey, Charles. *The Political Economy of Urban Poverty.* New York: Norton, 1973.

Schultz, Theodore W. *The Economic Value of Education.* New York: Columbia University Press, 1963.

Sexton, Patricia. *Education and Income: The Inequalities of Opportunity in Our Public Schools.* New York: Viking Press, 1964.

Silberman, Charles E. *Crisis in the Classroom: The Remaking of American Education.* New York: Random House, Inc., 1970.

Solman, Lewis, and Paul Taubman, eds. *Does College Make a Difference?* New York: Seminar Press, 1973.

Spring, Joel H. *Education and the Rise of the Corporate State.* Boston: Beacon Press, 1972.

Tabb, William K. *The Political Economy of the Black Ghetto.* New York: Norton, 1970.

The Task Force on Children out of School. *The Way We Go to School: The Exclusion of the Children in Boston.* Boston: Beacon Press, 1971.

Walberg, Herbert J., and Andrew T. Kopan, eds. *Rethinking Urban Education.* San Francisco: Jossey-Bass, Inc., Publishers, 1972.

Wise, Arthur E. *Rich Schools, Poor Schools: The Promise of Equal Educational Opportunity.* Chicago: University of Chicago Press, 1968.

Witty, Paul A., ed. *The Educationally Retarded and Disadvantaged.* Sixty-sixth Yearbook of the National Society for the Study of Education, Part I. Chicago: University of Chicago Press, 1967.

Wright, Nathan, Jr., ed. *What Black Educators Are Saying.* New York: Hawthorn Books, 1970.

Articles

Armor, David. "The Evidence on Busing," *The Public Interest,* No. 28 (Summer 1972), 90-126.

Bell, David, Daniel P. Moynihan, and Seymour Lipset, eds. "On Equality," *The Public Interest,* No. 29 (Fall 1972).

Bowles, Samuel. "Schooling and Inequality from Generation to Generation," *Journal of Political Economy,* Vol. 80 (May-June 1972), S219-51.

Epps, Edgar G., issue ed. "The Future of Education for Black Americans," *School Review,* Vol. 81 (May 1973), entire issue.

Gintis, Herbert. "Education, Technology and the Characteristics of Worker Productivity," *American Economic Review,* Vol. 61 (May 1971), 266-79.

Glazer, Nathan. "Is Busing Necessary?" *Commentary,* Vol. 53 (March. 1952), 39-52.

————. "The Limits of Social Policy," *Commentary,* Vol. 52 (September 1971), 51-58.

Goodall, Kenneth. "The Anti-Busing Paper—Wayward and Wrong." *Psychology Today,* Vol. 6 (November 1972) 42-44.

Green, Thomas F. "The Dismal Future of Equal Educational Opportunity," in Thomas F. Green, ed., *Educational Planning and Perspectives: Forecasting and Policy Making.* New York: IPC (America), Inc., 1971.

Guthrie, James W. "What the Coleman Reanalysis Didn't Tell Us," *Saturday Review,* Vol. 55 (July 22, 1972), 45.

Harvard Educational Review editors. "Perspectives on *Inequality: A Reassessment of the Effect of Family and Schooling in America,*" *Harvard Educational Review,* Vol. 43 (February 1973), 37-164. Articles are by Philip W. Jackson, Alice M. Rivlin, Ronald Edmonds *et al.,* Stephan Michelson, Lester C. Thurow, Kenneth B. Clark, Beverly Duncan, James S. Coleman, and a concluding comment by Christopher Jencks.

Havighurst, Robert J. "Minority Subcultures and the Law of Effect," *American Psychologist,* Vol. 25 (April 1970), 313-22.

Howe, Harold, II, issue ed. "Equal Educational Opportunity," *Harvard Educational Review,* Vol. 38 (Winter 1968), 3-175.

Hubert, Dick. "The Duluth Experience," *Saturday Review,* Vol. 55 (May 27, 1972), 55-58.

Jensen, Arthur R. "How Much Can We Boost IQ and Scholastic Achievement?" *Harvard Educational Review,* Vol. 39 (Winter 1969), 1-123. See also "Discussion: How Much Can We Boost IQ and Scholastic Achievement?" *Harvard Educational Review,* Vol. 39 (Spring 1969) for comments by Jerome S. Kagan, J. McV. Hunt, James F. Crow, Carl Bereiter, David Elkind, Lee J. Cronbach, and William F. Brazziel.

Lazerson, Marvin. "Revisionism and American Educational History," *Harvard Educational Review,* Vol. 43 (May 1973), 269-83.

Schockley, William. "Dysgenics, Geneticity, Raceology," *Phi Delta Kappan,* Vol. 53 (January 1972), 297-307.

Schoettle, Ferdinand P. "The Equal Protection Clause in Public Education," *Columbia Law Review,* Vol. 71 (December 1971), 1355-1419.

Stone, I. F. "The Politics of Busing," *New York Review of Books* (April 5, 1972).

Thurow, Lester C. "Education and Economic Equality," *The Public Interest,* No. 28 (Summer 1972), 66-80.

Wachtel, Howard M., and Charles Betsey. "Employment at Low Wages," *Review of Economics and Statistics,* Vol. 54 (March 1972), 121-29.

Wasserman, M. "The Contradictions of Anti-Busing and the Politics of Busing," *Liberation,* Vol. 17 (September 1972), 14-21.